The Craft of Palmistry

Five Element Chirology

And

Cross Referencing Hands - Traits A - Z

Published by MUSE PRESS

jen@cheiro.co.za
www.godgivenglyphs.com

ISBN: 9781983104558

With Gratitude

These books were gathered rather than written. I have compiled the interpretations from hundreds of sources over many years. To my teachers and to all whose palmistry books and articles have guided me, thank you.

In between the ideas and interpretations that came so long before mine, are the inspired threads, with which I weave my brand of understanding and teaching. Welcome to the gentle, powerful counseling, coaching and healing modality that is chirology.

For my beloved children, Adam, Nandita, and Kelly.

Contents

Part One

Part Two Cross Referencing Hands

Part One

The Craft

of

Palmistry

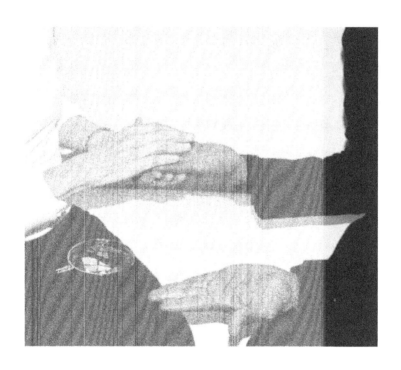

Five Element Chirology

Palm Printing

Collecting palm prints is an essential part of a Cheirologer's work. It is possible to read from the hand directly, but a print will give you a more definitively clear representation of the dermatoglyphics, lines and markings. Keep the prints filed in alphabetical order. The markings may change, and if you print the same hands in future years, you can spot the differences.

Materials

One ink roller - 10cm width works well
Water soluble block printing ink, e.g. ROLFES
White paper - 70-80gms recommended weight
Tile or piece of glass
Pen or pencil
Newspaper

i.   Place a few layers of newspaper onto a table, and position the tile, ink, roller and plain white paper on the newspaper.

ii.   Hands must be clean, dry and free of jewellery. Stroke the palmar surface and assess the skin texture. Earth and Fire skin need more ink than Water or Air skin texture.

iii.   Squeeze a small amount of ink onto the tile, and use the roller to spread the ink evenly over the tile or glass surface.

iv.   Take one of your friends' hands and apply the ink to it, using long strokes, as well as working the ink into the deeper folds and lines on their hand.

v.   Ask them to place their hand onto the sheet of paper. Make sure their hand is relaxed, aligned with the wrist, and in its most natural position. If you wish, draw an outline of the hand. Gently press at the base of the fingers and between the thumb and forefinger to ensure contact, and ask them to lift their hand.

vi.   Alternatively, to ensure that the hollow of the palm is clearly printed, slide the paper (and the hand) off the edge of the table and press upwards from beneath with your fingertips, into the hollow of the hand. Peel off the paper from under the hand.

vii.   Make sure that the thumb tip phalange is inked, and ask them to press just their thumb. If you wish, outline the thumb. Without allowing any rolling movement, let them lift their thumb.

viii.   Repeat this process with the other hand.

Always write the name, today's date, date of birth, and whether they are right or left hand active. Other relevant information would be: skin type, scars, moles, warts, nail shapes, hair, flexibility etc. or anything else that seems significant to you.

About Cheirology

The term Cheirology comes from the Greek word 'kheri' - 'hand' and 'ology' - 'knowledge of'. Cheirology embraces some of the rich depth of traditional western Palmistry's hundreds of years of ascribed astrological symbolism, but is more specifically based upon an ancient Chinese five-element system of interpreting the various shapes and forms of the hands.

Hand reading is a craft that incorporates both science and art. The craft of weaving provides a good analogy through which to describe the component parts of the work of the palm reader.

The loom around which the fabric of healing and service is woven is the dependable five element system of interpretation, called 'the language of the elements', which is based upon the hundreds of principles and characteristics of the four natural elements of Earth, Water, Fire and Air, and of our life force, Ether. This scientific system provides structure, context and source for the practitioner.

The texture of a Cheirology session is enriched with the healing touch, through which a blend of compassion, empathy, sensitivity and forgiveness is channelled. Loving kindness is really the primary remedy of our profession.

Our 'colours' are mixed as we endeavour, with as articulate explanations as we can manage, to illuminate those whose hands we hold, and the integrative binding threads of the weaving are the principles associated with Ether, the divine, subtle and intangible energy that permeates all life. Developing intuitive perception, the divinatory aspect of hand reading, is reliant upon offering ourselves as channels, symbolised by Ether.

Our focussed intention aids the evolution of the artistry and design of the therapy. The wider and deeper you journey toward understanding element resonance, the more articulately you will be able to weave the images that most clearly reflect aspects of human nature. Our needs, aspirations, strengths and weaknesses are all fashioned on our hands!

This book is an introduction to an intricate craft. For each marking shown, just a few of the possible associated meanings, gathered from years of research and practical hand reading experience, are suggested. I cannot over emphasise how important it is to find two or three markings that verify the accuracy of your interpretation, rather than come to a conclusion based upon one marking only. Explanations are presented in Part Two "Cross Referencing - Traits A –Z" of this book.

The 5 Elements

Understanding the principles of the 5 Elements is integral to Cheirology. Throughout this book, each element is presented with an associated glyph and colour. An orange square represents Earth, a blue circle represents Water, a red triangle represents Fire, a green cup represents Air, and a purple teardrop represents Ether.

For owners of black only printers, the shape of the glyph will determine the element rulership of each palmar marking.

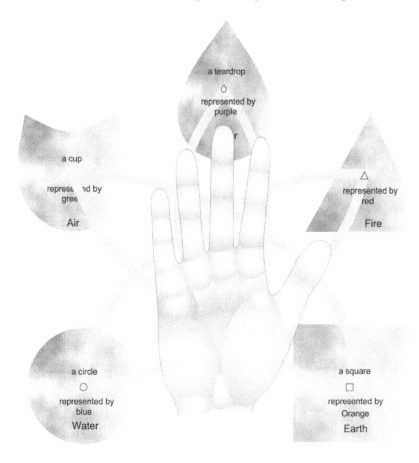

a teardrop

Ö

represented by
purple

a cup

repres   ed by
gree

Air

represented by
red

Fire

a circle

O

represented by
blue

Water

a square

□

represented by
Orange

Earth

The Healing Touch

Other than within applied physical therapies and healing techniques, there are no dialogue counselling modalities as intimate as Cheirology. Having your hands gently held, supported and stroked during a Cheirology session is comforting, relaxing and healing.

Being touched should give a sense of safety and nurturing, but beginner hand readers may lack confidence about how to hold the hands. Take the person's hands in yours, in a natural, comfortable and reassuring way. If the hands are offered with the palms facing downward, the person is more private or shy, and more reticent about exposing themselves.

Their right hand is in your left hand, and their left hand is in your right hand. This connection of positive and negative polarities creates a circuit of energy. Feel the current of energy running between you. If you have trained in Reiki or another energy healing technique, use your knowledge and experience. Breathe deeply, relax your back and allow energy to flow from you to them. Imagine that you are grounded to both the earth and the cosmos, so as to become a channel for universal source energy. Trying to be the source of the love and intention that pour from you will be too draining. With consciousness, Cheirologers can channel or direct energy towards any physical, mental or emotional need.

Stroke the skin, perhaps around the mounts, as you evaluate or explain the significance of each area. Flex the fingers and thumb, or do any other naturally flowing massage stroke.

During the reading it will feel appropriate to release the person's hands at times, but always gently take their hands in yours towards the end of the session. Be sure to be holding their hands as you bring the reading to closure.

Elements of a Cheirology Practice

The work of a Cheirologer is multi-dimensional. Along with learning about the meanings of the palmar markings, are other important levels of insight and awareness that develop concurrently.

Every aspect of the development of a Cheirology practice is also governed by principles of the elements. By combining the suggestions listed below, you are assured of a context within which to be of service.

'thread'
detached compassion
channelling
intuitive perception
non-judgement
wisdom

Ether level

'design
development of vocabulary
attentive listening
communication
analysis
objectivity
being observant
impartiality
research
optional recording device

Air level

'colours'
will, courage
& initiative!
defined direction
enthusiasm
print taking
creativity

Fire level

'texture'
service orientation
subjective understanding of emotions
fascination for the craft
love
forgiveness
sensitivity
empathy
caring

Water level

'Loom'
Study of morphology (form & markings)
history of hand reading
ethics of counselling
standards of conduct
methods of record keeping
scientific factors
humility
touch

Earth level

Professional Conduct

Assure your client of confidentiality, and make certain that there is no ambiguity regarding the fee for the session. Tell them that there will be no fortune telling and that the emphasis will be on identifying their optimal potentials. Explain that this is a dialogue therapy, and that they will gain most benefit if they participate and give feedback.

Hold eye contact when not looking at the palm or print, and don't allow distractions, such as answering the telephone, eating during the session etc. Be focussed and present and pay attention. Maintain sexual boundaries. Cheirology is a very intimate therapy, and attraction may occur - be respectful and contained.

Cheirology is a short-term intervention therapy that can have profound and deep impact. It may not be possible to have everything resolved by the end of the consultation, so ensure that the client is aware of your availability for further consultations to focus on the specific issues that have been identified.

If they are interested, it may be helpful to explain a little about elemental principle and how we interpret the hands.

Which Hand do we Read?

We read both hands, as both represent you as you are in the present. The active hand represents the conscious mind, the patterns most likely to continue, and the behaviour that you have greater awareness of. This is the hand used to write with.

The passive hand reflects the subconscious mind, inherited psychological and physiological traits and formative influences. Instinctive emotional responses, deeper desires and potential qualities that lie hidden and latent are also aspected.

Noticeable differences between the markings of the active and passive hands reveal conflicts between outer expression and inner needs. If your passive hand has clear lines, and the lines on your active hand are of poor quality, you have not used your potential. If the markings of your passive hand are messy and your active hand is clearer, negative circumstances have or will be overcome.

Language of the Elements

The principles of Ether, blended with the principles of Earth, Water, Fire and Air, form the 'loom', and provide the structure of the craft. It is from within a rich vocabulary of principles, qualities and characteristics that Cheirology's interpretive 'language' is sourced. Words are chosen to weave our intention, which is to hold, to heal and to illuminate those who offer us their hands. Some of the many principles that resonate with the five elements are suggested on this page. Each element is an aspect of Ether, vibrating at a different frequency, and manifesting in graded levels of materiality. Solid Earth has form and can be touched, receptive Water has no form yet may be touched, active Fire has no form, nor may it be touched, and intangible Air has no form. And Ether resides within Earth, Water, Fire and Air.

It is from within a rich vocabulary of principles is sourced. Words are chosen to weave our intention, which is to hold, to heal and to illuminate those who offer us their hands. Some of the many principles that resonate with the five elements are suggested on this page.

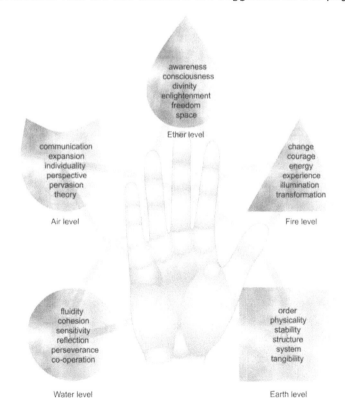

awareness
consciousness
divinity
enlightenment
freedom
space

Ether level

communication
expansion
individuality
perspective
pervasion
theory

Air level

change
courage
energy
experience
illumination
transformation

Fire level

fluidity
cohesion
sensitivity
reflection
perseverance
co-operation

Water level

order
physicality
stability
structure
system
tangibility

Earth level

Qualities of the Elements

Our vocabulary expands as we understand that every imaginable human trait expresses either one, or a combination of elements. Here are some positive and negative examples of what someone with Earth, Water, Fire, Air or Ether palmar markings might be like.

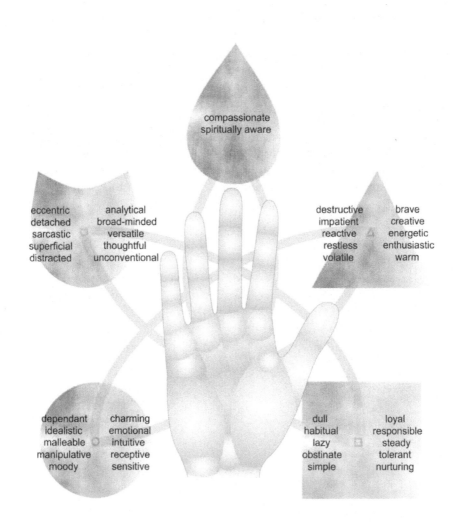

compassionate
spiritually aware

eccentric   analytical
detached   broad-minded
sarcastic   versatile
superficial   thoughtful
distracted   unconventional

destructive   brave
impatient   creative
reactive   energetic
restless   enthusiastic
volatile   warm

dependant   charming
idealistic   emotional
malleable   intuitive
manipulative   receptive
moody   sensitive

dull   loyal
habitual   responsible
lazy   steady
obstinate   tolerant
simple   nurturing

10

Counselling

As a counselling modality and a dialogue therapy, Cheirology identifies five realms of human experience. Governed by element principles, the balanced inter-relationship of physical (Earth), emotional (Water), vocational (Fire), intellectual (Air) and spiritual (Ether) functions, are each integral to optimal happiness.

By the end of the hand reading session, the component parts of each realm will have had mention. This structured approach forms the context for Cheirological counselling, ensuring that the reading is not a random hit and miss affair.

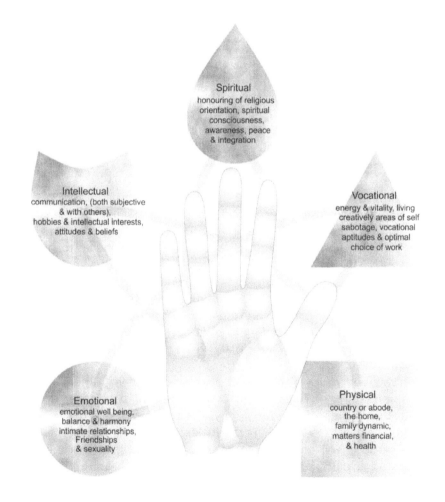

Spiritual
honouring of religious
orientation, spiritual
consciousness,
awareness, peace
& integration

Intellectual
communication, (both subjective
& with others),
hobbies & intellectual interests,
attitudes & beliefs

Vocational
energy & vitality, living
creatively areas of self
sabotage, vocational
aptitudes & optimal
choice of work

Emotional
emotional well being,
balance & harmony
intimate relationships,
Friendships
& sexuality

Physical
country or abode,
the home,
family dynamic,
matters financial,
& health

Intuition

Psychic and intuitive skills have always been a part of the hand reading craft. With a grounding in the study of the principles of Cheirology, attunement to images, metaphors, colours, sensations and impressions increase, as if this inexplicable part of our work has a life of its own!

Intuitive perception has nothing to do with intellect and analysis. Information is felt, seen or heard, somewhere inside, somewhere instinctive, and then only is it thought about. Intuition is the wisdom of a knowing that is more senior than belief. 'Knowing' comes from soul, spirit and heart. Belief is an action of thought, and comes from the mind. Intuition cannot be learned through will, but can only be received, through being willing.

To read more intuitively, state your intention, and ask your Higher Self for guidance and assistance to expand awareness. Ask for permission to be used as a channel for information, healing and love. Self-enquiry, or checking in with where you are at personally, will help prevent any links or projections from your own emotional climate.

Take time before your consultation to meditate and to breathe, so as to be as relaxed and centred as possible. Breathing is a key to relaxation, and being relaxed helps open channels for intuitive perception.

Sit with your friend, hold their hands, and look into their eyes. Without necessarily losing eye contact, imagine that your third eye, the sixth chakra centre in the middle of your forehead, can see. Scan with this 'eye' up, down and around their body, and you will begin to sense differences in their energy field. Look at their hands and see if any areas of the palmar surface 'talk' to you.

You can also 'look' with other energy centres. The second chakra, below the navel, is a sensitive receptor for information, as is the heart. If the person who you are tuning in to is not physically present, scan their palm prints, and allow your body to be receptive and responsive in the same way.

Be attentive to subtle nuances of possible sensations, emotions, or visual impressions of colour, light or darkness in their body, or on areas of their palms. If you feel a physical symptom, does the feeling inside you contract or expand? Is the feeling empty and deficient, or is there a sense of fullness, or excess? Is it hot or cold, tingly, painful, creepy, light or dark, heavy, hostile, nauseating or exhilarating? These are just a few of a range of infinite possibilities.

our slightest bodily sensation or mental image can be linked to their physical, emotional, mental, and spiritual circumstances. For example, does a tingling sensation in your solar plexus indicate that they are excited, or are they anxious? Your inner voice of knowing will answer.

As with every aspect of hand reading, only share your impressions if you are certain that it is ethical and appropriate to articulate the information.

Handshake

Handshakes fall somewhere on the scale between limp fish and bone crusher. Soft handshakes can show lack of energy, selfishness and insincerity. It is as if the person has barely enough interest in you to greet you. But take care not to come to any negative conclusion before you have intuitively 'scanned' to 'see' whether they are perhaps ill, or distressed. If the hand is moist, depression, emotional crisis and reduced coping skills are possible.

A firm handshake from someone with dry skin (Fire element influence) hints at practical energy and vitality. The person is pragmatic, and may be sceptical of all but 'the tried and the true'. A firm shake (Fire / Earth element influence) from a moist hand (Water element influence) indicates emotional sensitivity, anxiety, vulnerability and stress, yet the firmness shows enough underlying determination to overcome difficulties.

Occasionally the bone-crushing hand shaker is genuinely so full of the joy of life that they do not realize how strong they are. They are completely out of touch. However, they are more likely to be arrogant, controlling, insensitive, 'thick skinned' and rude. Spiritual refinement is reduced. The person could be in denial about aspects of their life that are out of control. Consider the possibility of misogyny if it is a man, or cruelty.

If someone holds your hand longer than necessary they want something, or are seductively signalling attraction.

Note: Different cultures have associated styles of handshakes, these must be taken into consideration before making your assessment.

Consistency

The consistency of the hand can be assessed during a handshake. If hands are soft, energy is lessened, effort cannot be sustained, and physical activity is not particularly enjoyed. Indolence and self-indulgence are likely, although soft handed people are also astute or even shrewd.

A hard hand, which has no 'give' to the flesh, shows the energetic, hardworking realist. Emotions may be repressed however, and the hard-handed prefer to get on with life rather than to emotionally 'excavate' too deeply.

Colour of the Palms

Variations of colour of the hands indicate emotional and personality traits. Red palms aspect energy and enthusiasm. A blue tinge shows moodiness and possible self-destructiveness. Yellow palms signal the cranky pessimist. Pale hands show self-centredness, idealism and lack of energy. White palms aspect the selfish person who dislikes demands being made upon them. Vitality is lacking, and possibly they are ill. Pink is the ideal colour for health, balance and congeniality.

Size of the Hands

The size of the hands only has relevance if the hands appear big, or small, in relation to the height and size of their bearer. Large handed people are methodical and thorough. Often found on those who do precision work, these people are patient and persevering, but tend to have slow, considered responses. Time is wasted on unnecessary details, and the large handed dislike rushing and sudden changes.

Small hands in relation to height show a lively and alert person with quick, impulsive responses and an instinctive sense of how to delegate, manage and handle any emergency. They are impatient, intolerant of others' relative slowness, are easily distracted and do not pay attention to details.

Gesticulation

By observing what people do with their hands, e.g. keeping them in pockets, holding them behind their backs, splaying them out onto the table in front of them as they sit down on a chair, sit on them etc., you will begin, with the aid of your intuition, to develop your own repertoire of insights as to what the gesture signals.

Expressive and expansive hand movements show a more extrovert and optimistic soul, whereas reserved movements indicate a more guarded, fearful and rigid outlook. The person does not want to expose him or herself. Wringing of the hands shows worry and nervous strain, and holding the thumbs indicates anxiety and temporary lack of confidence.

The Chart of the Hand

The hand is divided vertically by drawing a line from the middle of the tip of the Earth finger to the mid-point of the base of the hand (A - A). The thumb side is the radial side, which represents the outer and conscious self, and the baby finger side is called the ulnar side, representing the inner, unconscious self.

Quadrants are the four areas that are defined after a vertical and horizontal division, i.e. a cross, has been superimposed onto the palm. To quadrant, measure the distance from the base of the Earth finger to the base of the hand, along the same vertical division described above, i.e. drawn from the tip of the middle finger to the mid-point at the base of the hand (B - B). Using a protractor, draw a bilateral division at the mid-point (C - C).

Each of the four quadrants is associated with an element. If a quadrant is particularly large or small, the accorded elemental influence in the bearers' character increases or decreases respectively.

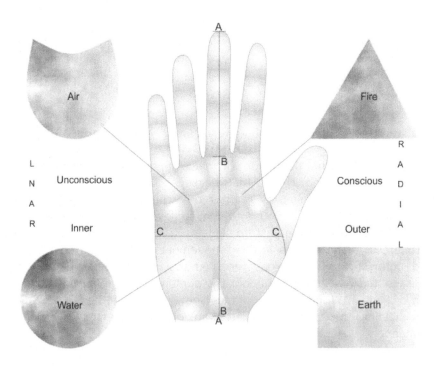

Skin Texture

There are four types of skin texture. Each has an associated element, showing something of our deepest responses to the world. Our skin is the membrane through which we receive, and reflects our 'element of impression', giving clues as to the environment to which we are best suited.

To determine the skin texture, lightly run your fingertips over the palm of the hand. If different skin textures are present on one hand, the interpretations are blended together. The person is attuned to, and comfortable in more than one type of atmosphere.

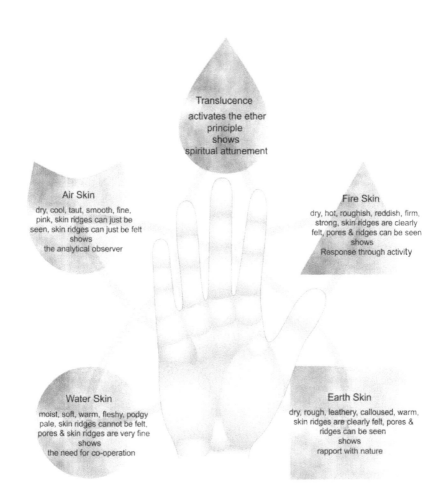

Translucence
activates the ether
principle
shows
spiritual attunement

Air Skin
dry, cool, taut, smooth, fine,
pink, skin ridges can just be
seen, skin ridges can just be felt
shows
the analytical observer

Fire Skin
dry, hot, roughish, reddish, firm,
strong, skin ridges are clearly
felt, pores & ridges can be seen
shows
Response through activity

Water Skin
moist, soft, warm, fleshy, podgy
pale, skin ridges cannot be felt,
pores & skin ridges are very fine
shows
the need for co-operation

Earth Skin
dry, rough, leathery, calloused, warm,
skin ridges are clearly felt, pores &
ridges can be seen
shows
rapport with nature

Hand Shape

Four archetypes, the earthy, watery, fiery or airy type of person, are represented in four basic hand shapes. We resonate with and express ourselves through qualities associated with Earth, Water, Fire and Air. Principles and characteristics associated with each of these elements provide the source for personality profiles. Your hand shape tells of your 'element of expression'.

Identifying the archetypes, and understanding the associated traits within yourself, is the first basic step before you can begin to blend in the influences from other markings.

Ether

has no associated hand shape

Air is weightless; it has no tangible source & is the most ineffable & indefinable element. We cannot see or describe formless, shapeless, invisible Air, yet we can feel the effect of how it penetrates as we breathe it into our bodies. Pervasion is one of many Air principles, suggesting that the Air archetype penetrates beyond the apparent their search for understanding

Unlike the receptive, yin elements of Earth and Water, Fire has no form & can never be still. Fire moves & seeks, outward & upward, & consumes & transforms all it meets by turning what it encounters into more of itself. Fire brings change, & makes way for the future two of the many principles with which the Fire archetype resonates are activity & energy

The flow of the Water element within us senses & imagines life's possibilities, feels inspired & 'gets carried away'. In nature, Water also has determination & perseverance. Water archetypes are sensitive, emotional & adaptable, & have many other traits associated with the Water element

The Earth is solid & reliable & generates a comforting, nurturing energy that anchors us with a sense of structure, safety & security. Dependability steadiness, & many other traits that resonate with the natural functions of Earth are ascribed to the Earth archetype

Determining Hand Shape

Are the hands Earth, Water, Fire or Air shaped? To decide, we assess the shape of the palm, and the relative length of the fingers. Palms are either square or oblong. In relation to the palm, fingers are either short or long.

Each of the four handshape types have many associated responsive, redeemed and positive attributes, as well as potential reactive, unredeemed or negative characteristics of temperament. Some examples are shown on the next four pages.

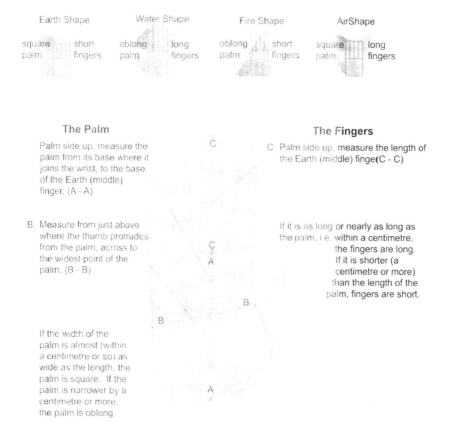

Earth Shape   Water Shape   Fire Shape   AirShape

square · short   oblong · long   oblong · short   square · long
palm · fingers   palm · fingers   palm · fingers   palm · fingers

The Palm

Palm side up, measure the palm from its base where it joins the wrist, to the base of the Earth (middle) finger. (A - A)

B. Measure from just above where the thumb protrudes from the palm, across to the widest point of the palm. (B - B)

If the width of the palm is almost (within a centimetre or so) as wide as the length, the palm is square. If the palm is narrower by a centimetre or more, the palm is oblong.

The Fingers

C. Palm side up, measure the length of the Earth (middle) finger(C - C)

If it is as long or nearly as long as the palm, i.e. within a centimetre, the fingers are long. If it is shorter (a centimetre or more) than the length of the palm, fingers are short.

Earth Shaped Hand

The Earth person is happiest in an enduring traditional relationship. Domestic harmony is fundamental for their well-being. What hurts them most is violation of trust, and betrayals will never be forgotten. Simplicity, routine, mealtimes with the family and material security give the earthy type peace.

They are strong in physique and constitution and are seldom ill, yet have a general predisposition to digestive disorders due to the burying of negative emotions. Self-enquiry is avoided and reflection and insight are blocked and hidden from themselves and others. Analysis, intellectualising and investigation do not form a part of their response to living, and they are often rather quiet and uncommunicative, unless the discussion is of a purely practical nature.

Earth people are suited to working in longstanding positions that provide support and security for both themselves and others. Examples of these are farming, food and catering, building, government or civil service.

Spiritually they adhere to the traditional belief systems followed by their father and his father before.

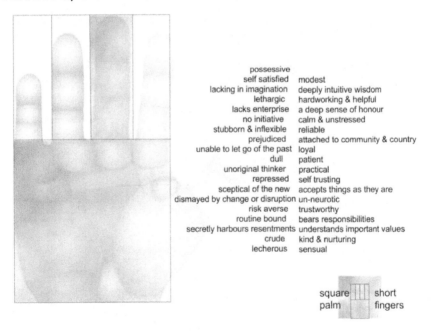

possessive	
self satisfied	modest
lacking in imagination	deeply intuitive wisdom
lethargic	hardworking & helpful
lacks enterprise	a deep sense of honour
no initiative	calm & unstressed
stubborn & inflexible	reliable
prejudiced	attached to community & country
unable to let go of the past	loyal
dull	patient
unoriginal thinker	practical
repressed	self trusting
sceptical of the new	accepts things as they are
dismayed by change or disruption	un-neurotic
risk averse	trustworthy
routine bound	bears responsibilities
secretly harbours resentments	understands important values
crude	kind & nurturing
lecherous	sensual

square palm   short fingers

These character traits pertain to the shape of the hand, and can also be ascribed to Earth skin texture and to other markings ruled by the Earth element.

Water Shaped Hand

Water in nature flows towards and seeks cohesion with more water. The archetypal Water person seeks a romantic relationship, companionship and close involvement with friends. Platonic friendships may substitute for physical intimacy.

The less constitutionally robust Water types are predisposed to allergies, water retention, bladder and prostate problems, eczema and other skin ailments.

Discord distresses them. Best suited to working in harmonious and empathic environments, they are often found in healing and service professions, or networking in a public relations job. With innate style, flair and elegance, they are also suited to working in the art world, or in design and décor.

Water types have deep spiritual potential, and a natural connection to meditation. They are highly impressionable and intuitive, even psychic. An undeveloped subject may imagine too much and see or believe the sinister, whereas matters mystical could inspire a more conscious Water personality.

depressive	reflective
manipulative	susceptible to being manipulated
insecure, needy & clingy	nurturing
touchy	sensitive
idealistic	aspires
emotional & moody	shares feelings
evasive	receptive
egocentrically self absorbed	caring & empathic
melodramatic	still
subjective	imaginative
deceptive or devious	discreet
martyred	self sacrificing
seductive	charming
malleable	adaptable
illusionary	mystical
smothering	devoted
indecisive	flexible

oblong palm   long fingers

These character traits pertain to the shape of the hand, and can also be ascribed to Water skin texture and to other markings ruled by the Water element.

Fire Shaped Hand

Impatient with more subjectively emotional types, Fire types prefer dynamic partnerships. Shared activities, passionate sex and spontaneity are criteria for the foundation of relationship.

They generally have a vigorous metabolism and are constitutionally robust, but heart disease, high blood pressure and hot, feverish and inflammatory conditions are characterised, as fiery types become over stimulated and 'burn the candle at both ends'.

Ambitious and enterprising Fire people are found in positions in corporate, politics, sport or military. They are the ego centred and innovative leaders and project managers who strategize and make a difference. Creative artists who are influential in effecting progress and change are also expressing Fire energy.

The Fire person may have a fundamentalist approach to religion, with dogmatic fervour and intense need to effect change. They may be found or passionately engaged with transformational development training, or they may have no religious or spiritual orientation at all!

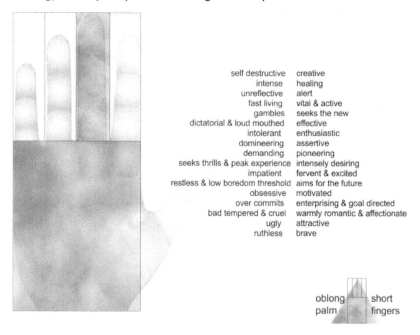

self destructive	creative
intense	healing
unreflective	alert
fast living	vital & active
gambles	seeks the new
dictatorial & loud mouthed	effective
intolerant	enthusiastic
domineering	assertive
demanding	pioneering
seeks thrills & peak experience	intensely desiring
impatient	fervent & excited
restless & low boredom threshold	aims for the future
obsessive	motivated
over commits	enterprising & goal directed
bad tempered & cruel	warmly romantic & affectionate
ugly	attractive
ruthless	brave

oblong palm   short fingers

These character traits pertain to the shape of the hand, and can also be ascribed to Fire skin texture and to other markings ruled by the Fire element.

Air Shaped Hand

Air people need space and independence, and feel hemmed in and trapped if restricted in any way. Their need for freedom brings the ability to detach emotionally. Feelings are intellectualised and rationalised or made light. Many air types choose to live alone, perhaps because intimacy threatens.

They are predisposed to insomnia, stress, anxiety, nervous disorders and respiratory problems. Stiffening of joints is characterised, due to worry and criticism.

Career paths chosen by those with Air shaped hands are often media related, and unconventional and individualistic. The archetypal absent-minded professor describes another Air type. He forgets to eat, and is in his element while researching, teaching and writing. Some Air people become lively and animated when communicating, and others have a more solitary disposition.

Air types are inclined towards concepts, ideologies or to an applied philosophy of understanding, e.g. Buddhism, rather than to a dogmatic prescribed religion or watery spiritual leaning.

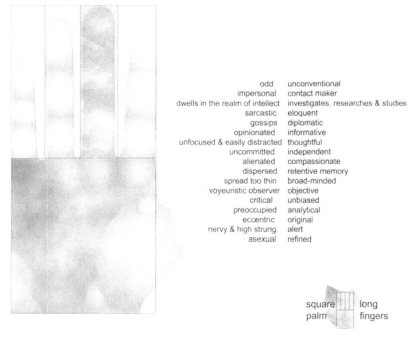

odd	unconventional
impersonal	contact maker
dwells in the realm of intellect	investigates, researches & studies
sarcastic	eloquent
gossips	diplomatic
opinionated	informative
unfocused & easily distracted	thoughtful
uncommitted	independent
alienated	compassionate
dispersed	retentive memory
spread too thin	broad-minded
voyeuristic observer	objective
critical	unbiased
preoccupied	analytical
eccentric	original
nervy & high strung	alert
asexual	refined

square palm   long fingers

These character traits pertain to the shape of the hand, and can also be ascribed to Air skin texture and to other markings ruled by the Air element.

Hand Shape Angles & Curves

These variations of the outline of the hand's structure are easy to spot and to remember. The associated meanings of these reliable and accurate interpretive indicators are drawn from the old lore of Palmistry.

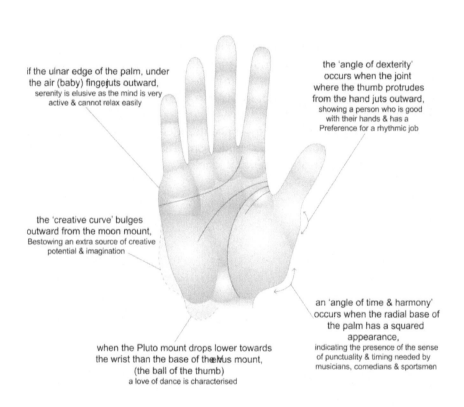

if the ulnar edge of the palm, under the air (baby) finger juts outward,
serenity is elusive as the mind is very active & cannot relax easily

the 'angle of dexterity' occurs when the joint where the thumb protrudes from the hand juts outward,
showing a person who is good with their hands & has a Preference for a rhythmic job

the 'creative curve' bulges outward from the moon mount,
Bestowing an extra source of creative potential & imagination

an 'angle of time & harmony' occurs when the radial base of the palm has a squared appearance,
indicating the presence of the sense of punctuality & timing needed by musicians, comedians & sportsmen

when the Pluto mount drops lower towards the wrist than the base of the Venus mount, (the ball of the thumb)
a love of dance is characterised

Mounts

Mounts are the fleshy pads that contour to a greater or lesser degree over the palm. They should appear slightly rounded, in harmonious proportion. To interpret them, we turn to ascribed planetary qualities, drawn from the ancient lore of astrology.

The mounts each store a capacity of potential energy. If the mount is noticeably large, or deficient, energies related to that mount are aspected. Large mounts are plump or full, showing an excess of associated energies. A deficient mount is flat, or even concave, showing a deficit of associated energies.

Each mount also resonates with an element. Some examples of the principles of the celestial bodies, their astrological symbol, and their element rulership, are diagrammed below.

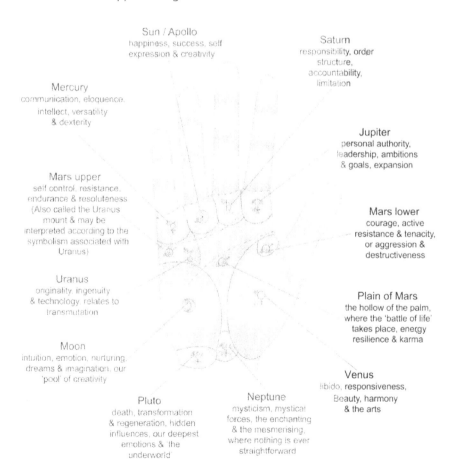

Sun / Apollo
happiness, success, self expression & creativity

Saturn
responsibility, order structure, accountability, limitation

Mercury
communication, eloquence, intellect, versatility & dexterity

Jupiter
personal authority, leadership, ambitions & goals, expansion

Mars upper
self control, resistance, endurance & resoluteness (Also called the Uranus mount & may be interpreted according to the symbolism associated with Uranus)

Mars lower
courage, active resistance & tenacity, or aggression & destructiveness

Uranus
originality, ingenuity & technology, relates to transmutation

Plain of Mars
the hollow of the palm, where the 'battle of life' takes place, energy resilience & karma

Moon
intuition, emotion, nurturing, dreams & imagination, our 'pool' of creativity

Venus
libido, responsiveness, Beauty, harmony & the arts

Pluto
death, transformation & regeneration, hidden influences, our deepest emotions & the underworld

Neptune
mysticism, mystical forces, the enchanting & the mesmerising, where nothing is ever straightforward

Digital Dermatoglyphics

We know that our fingerprints are a reliable means of identifying our individuality, but our dermatoglyphics (fingerprint patterns) also provide information about our different styles of conceptual thought, and of our mental predispositions.

Each dermatoglyphic ('derma' = skin, and 'glyph' = carving) pattern of the fingers and thumbs has an associated elemental resonance. Most people have combinations of dermatoglyphics on their fingertips, or they may have ten of the same pattern. A full set of loops is common, but a full set of whorls or arches are more rare. Tented Arches are seldom found on more than three of our ten fingers, and ten Double Loops would be a rare find indeed.

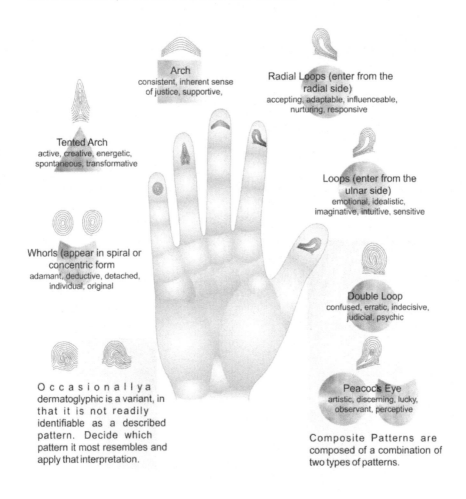

Arch
consistent, inherent sense of justice, supportive,

Radial Loops (enter from the radial side)
accepting, adaptable, influenceable, nurturing, responsive

Tented Arch
active, creative, energetic, spontaneous, transformative

Loops (enter from the ulnar side)
emotional, idealistic, imaginative, intuitive, sensitive

Whorls (appear in spiral or concentric form
adamant, deductive, detached, individual, original

Double Loop
confused, erratic, indecisive, judicial, psychic

Occasionally a dermatoglyphic is a variant, in that it is not readily identifiable as a described pattern. Decide which pattern it most resembles and apply that interpretation.

Peacock's Eye
artistic, discerning, lucky, observant, perceptive

Composite Patterns are composed of a combination of two types of patterns.

Palmar Dermatoglyphics

Dermatoglyphics (skin ridge patterns) are also found on the palmar surface. Dermatoglyphics most likely to be found on or between the mounts under the fingers are illustrated on this page, each with some possible interpretations.

Serious Intent loops
drop downward between the
Fire & Earth fingers, showing a
work ethic & a dislike of
frittering away time

Charisma loops
drop downward between the
Earth & Water fingers. Personal
magnetism & leadership abilities
are aspected

Style loops
lie diagonally over the Apollo mount under
the Fire finger Flair with colour, decor &
design, personal style, & concern with
appearance are indicated

Humour loops
drop downward between the
Air & Fire fingers, showing optimism
& a light & expansive view to life.
The person has a good sense of
humour, but this marking could also
aspect a cynical & sarcastic

Inter-digital whorls
are found pocketed within the Humour
& Serious Intent loops, & in rare cases are
spotted in a Charisma or Courage loop.
The Whorl overlays an Air influence of
detachment & individuality to the meanings
of the inter-digital loops. Inter-digital Whorls
between the Air & Fire fingers show that
humour & wit are used as a form of emotional
defence. An inter-digital Whorl between the
Fire & Earth fingers suggests a very refined
work ethic & an original career focus

Palmar Dermatoglyphics

The Courage loop, the Bee and the Music loop are occasionally found on the Mars and Venus mounts. These may appear in isolation, or two or even all three may be present on one hand. Whorls on the Venus mount are seldom found, and the Double loop in this position is extremely rare.

Triradii occur when three directions of skin ridges converge to create a small triangle. Governed by Fire, they appear on each digital mount and at the base of the hand (axial triradius).

The patterns are diagrammed on this page with some of their associated meanings.

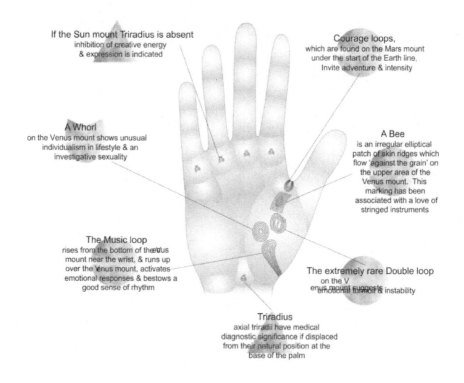

If the Sun mount Triradius is absent inhibition of creative energy & expression is indicated

Courage loops, which are found on the Mars mount under the start of the Earth line, Invite adventure & intensity

A Whorl on the Venus mount shows unusual individualism in lifestyle & an investigative sexuality

A Bee is an irregular elliptical patch of skin ridges which flow 'against the grain' on the upper area of the Venus mount. This marking has been associated with a love of stringed instruments

The Music loop rises from the bottom of the Venus mount near the wrist, & runs up over the Venus mount, activates emotional responses & bestows a good sense of rhythm

The extremely rare Double loop on the Venus mount suggests emotional turmoil & instability

Triradius axial triradii have medical diagnostic significance if displaced from their natural position at the base of the palm

Palmar Dermatoglyphics

There are an array of possible dermatoglyphic patterns which manifest on the ulnar side, on the Moon and Pluto mounts. The most common patterns are illustrated on this page, and some of the associated meanings are mentioned.

Memory loops
open from the radial side & flow over the
Moon mount, aspecting a love of water
attunement to others' emotional states,
good dream recall, & a deep memory of
non material realms of experience.
Intuition will be acute

Arch
a person with an arch
flowing over their Moon
mount has a constructive
& practical imagination

Bearers of Moon mount Whorls
are talented, gifted & unusual souls.
Their absolute singularity could be
expressed through art, acting or
teaching

**The unusual
Tented arch**
on a Moon mount
will increase
initiative,
enthusiasm
& vitality

A Double loop
on the Moon mount balances
masculine & feminine energies
& activates the intuition

The Empathy loop
rises from the base of the
wrist & runs upward & over
towards the Moon mount.
Compassion for others & an
inspired, visionary &
creative imagination is
aspected

The Nature loop
enters the Moon or Pluto
mount from the ulnar side.
The bearer has a love of
nature & animals & an
intuitive understanding of
natural cycles

Thumbs

The most important digit of the hand is the thumb. Traditionally called the 'ruler of the hand', the size, shape, flexibility, dermatoglyphic and setting indicate whether potentials indicated elsewhere in the hand can be realised or not.

Thumbs have only two phalanges. The lower phalange is ruled by Water and its form tells of how we rationalise, evaluate and reason. The tip of the thumb is Fire ruled, and its appearance describes how we apply our personal energy, volition, determination and will. The thumbs have no Air level. The Earth element is represented in the Venus mount (ball of the thumb - see Mounts.)

A strong thumb is long, firm and wide set, and these characteristics indicate determination. A weak thumb is short, flexible, high set and held close to the palm, characterising passivity and lack of follow through.

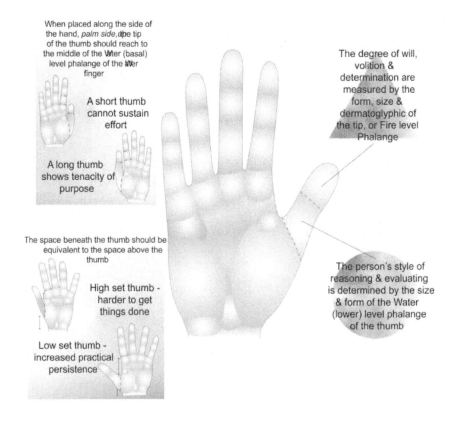

When placed along the side of the hand, *palm side,* the tip of the thumb should reach to the middle of the Water (basal) level phalange of the Water finger

A short thumb cannot sustain effort

A long thumb shows tenacity of purpose

The space beneath the thumb should be equivalent to the space above the thumb

High set thumb - harder to get things done

Low set thumb - increased practical persistence

The degree of will, volition & determination are measured by the form, size & dermatoglyphic of the tip, or Fire level Phalange

The person's style of reasoning & evaluating is determined by the size & form of the Water (lower) level phalange of the thumb

30

Thumb Shapes

A longer Water (lower) phalange indicates increased deliberation, evaluation, rationalization & 'analysis paralysis'

A longer Fire (tip) phalange indicates wilfulness, volition & impulsiveness. The person 'acts first & thinks later'

A stiff thumb increases self mastery & determination. The person may be unyielding & obstinate

A flexible thumb tip highlights adaptability but reduces focussed application

A hyper-flexive lower joint of the thumb indicates that others or circumstances are blamed for life's calamities, with an accompanying avoidance of taking responsibility

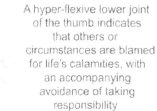

Selfishness & insecurity are indicated when the thumb tip bends inwards

A narrow angle between the thumb & the hand (less than 45°) indicates poor confidence & vulnerability

The wider the angle between the thumb & the hand, the more confident, assertive & forceful the personality

Thumb Shapes

A 'clubbed thumb' shows that pent up energy may explode violently (termed the 'murderer's thumb')

A spoke shaved thumb shows a determined, but manipulative use of will

Thickness increases practicality, capability & enterprise

The thinner the thumb, the more impractical the person

Thumb Tip Shapes

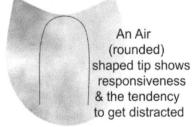

An Air (rounded) shaped tip shows responsiveness & the tendency to get distracted

A Fire (spatulate) shaped tip shows enthusiastic energy that could become dissipated

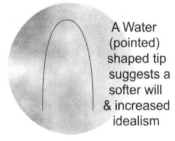

A Water (pointed) shaped tip suggests a softer will & increased idealism

An Earth (square) shaped tip shows good common sense & reliability

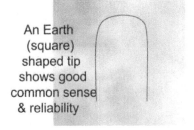

Fingers

The form of our fingers suggests something of our responses to life. Each finger has an element rulership, and each represents an area of life and has an ascribed 'identity'.

Earth rules the middle (Saturn) finger This is your finger of 'cultural identity'. Your sense of duty responsibilityorder, structure, & an inner point of balance & security are aspected

Water rules the index (Jupiter) finger This is your finger of 'personal identity'. Your relationship with yourself, your image & self esteem are Aspected

Fire rules the ring (Apollo) finger. This is your finger of extra personal identity.' Creative expression is aspected

Air rules the baby (Mercury) finger This is your finger of 'impersonal identity'. Communication, sexuality & financial Exchange are aspected

Ether principles govern the thumb, which is your digit of 'spiritual identity'. The generating energy of reason & the sustaining energy of will are aspected

Finger Spacing

Some people hold their fingers wide apart from one another especially when they speak, and others tend to hold their fingers more tightly Together

Fingers held wide apart
optimism, extroversion & free spiritedness are some of the associated traits

Fingers held tightly together
reserve, apprehension & lack of spontaneity are some of the associated traits

Finger Length

Long fingers (found on Water & Air shaped hands) show patience, concern for detail and a more analytical orientation. Short fingers (found on Earth & Fire shaped hands) show a practical, impatient and impulsive person.

The fingers are also assessed in relation to each other. The relatively largest finger shows which element and aspect of life is most predominantly emphasised in the person's life. If a finger is too small, the element is underutilised.

Also take into consideration that the true length of the fingers may be disguised by the setting, that is, the level from which they protrude from the palm.

The Air finger should reach the inter-phalangeal crease between the Fire & Air phalanges of the Fire finger

The Water & Fire fingers should be the same length as each other i.e. reaching half way to the top phalange of the Earth finger

The Earth finger is short if it is less than half a phalange length longer than the lengths of the (normal Length) Water & Fire fingers

Phalanges

The three bones of each of the fingers, and the two protruding bones of the thumbs, are called phalanges. The phalanges closest to the palm are the basal phalanges, and they are governed by Water principles. The middle level phalanges are governed by Fire principles, and the fingertips are governed by Air principles. The fingers have no earth level phalanges.

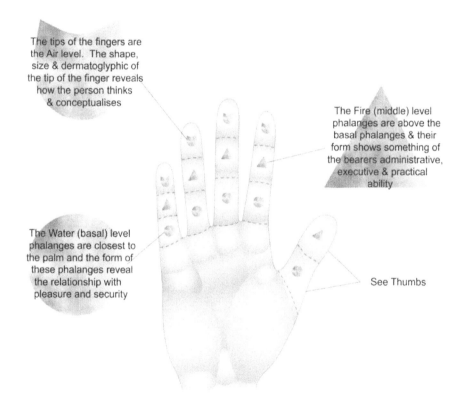

The tips of the fingers are the Air level. The shape, size & dermatoglyphic of the tip of the finger reveals how the person thinks & conceptualises

The Fire (middle) level phalanges are above the basal phalanges & their form shows something of the bearers administrative, executive & practical ability

The Water (basal) level phalanges are closest to the palm and the form of these phalanges reveal the relationship with pleasure and security

See Thumbs

Finger Form

Thick fingers show practicality. The person exposes themselves to life, has a robust constitution, & enjoys the material world of physical contact, sex & food. There may be a course side to the nature

Thin fingers show less practicality & more idealism, sensitivity & refinement. Life is more threatening

increasing deliberation, examination & analysis. Spontaneity is restricted. Mental & physical expression is slower & more careful. Knots are found on philosophical souls who have deep rooted convictions, concern for detail & who can work systematically

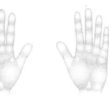

Smooth fingers show that mental energy flows uninterrupted & that intuition is more spontaneous. There is a dislike for protracted analysis

Flexible fingers show a responsively open mind, adaptability & receptivity If they are too supple, gullibility & lack of discrimination increase

Stiff fingers (Earth / Fire influence) show fixed adherence to patterns or traditions, cautious scepticism & resistance to the unconventional. Stiff fingered people may have a greater degree of self mastery

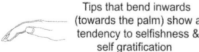

Tips that bend inwards (towards the palm) show a tendency to selfishness & self gratification

Tips that turn up at their ends show an entertaining, funny person, who has the ability to mimic & the inability to keep a secret!

36

Fingertip Shapes

Fingertip shapes reveal how the energy within the identity of that finger is expressed in the world. Each is interpreted according to the area of life represented by that finger. If hands have different shaped tips on each of their fingers, combine the meaning of the shape of the tip, with the qualities associated with that finger, or base your analysis upon the shape that is most predominant.

Earth shaped tips are squarish showing practical common sense. The optimal shape for the administrative worker but order & methodical ways will restrict spontaneity

Fire shaped tips are spatulate & reveal enterprise, enthusiasm & energy that could become obsessive or lack focus

Water shaped tips taper to a point aspecting sensitivity & intuition, shadowed by impracticality & idealism

Air shaped tips are conic or rounded, showing a perceptive, responsive & spontaneous communicator & thinker

Ether has no associated

Finger Bends

It has been said that 'fingers are best worn straight', however, many people have one or more fingers that bend this way or that. The energy associated with the bending finger is not flowing optimally.

Here are four of the possible ways that fingers might bend, along with just a few of the many associated meanings.

Air bends to Fire
a slight bend shows a persuasive, diplomatic & tactful communicator
A sharp bend shows shrewdness, insincerity, fondness for intrigue & the tendency to manipulate communication channels for vested interests

Fire bends to Earth
shows the need for a profession, boredom with domesticity & the likelihood of a sense of duty inhibiting their happiness

Water bends to Earth
shows lack of confidence, emotional acquisitiveness & a history of exposure to injustice

Earth bends to Fire
indicates exposure to double standards in childhood resulting in rebelliousness, difficulty in coping with responsibility & the need for alone time

Nail Shapes

There are four main nail shapes and each shape is governed by an element. The shape of your nails indicates the element through which you most habitually project yourself. Various health conditions are also revealed in the shapes of and markings on the nails.

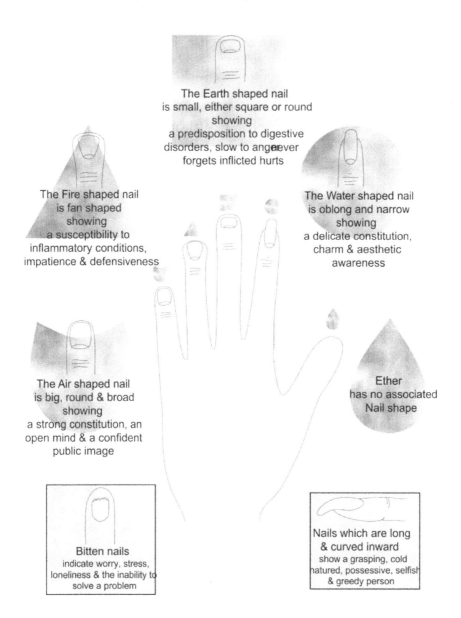

The Earth shaped nail
is small, either square or round
showing
a predisposition to digestive
disorders, slow to anger ever
forgets inflicted hurts

The Fire shaped nail
is fan shaped
showing
a susceptibility to
inflammatory conditions,
impatience & defensiveness

The Water shaped nail
is oblong and narrow
showing
a delicate constitution,
charm & aesthetic
awareness

The Air shaped nail
is big, round & broad
showing
a strong constitution, an
open mind & a confident
public image

Ether
has no associated
Nail shape

Bitten nails
indicate worry, stress,
loneliness & the inability to
solve a problem

Nails which are long
& curved inward
show a grasping, cold
natured, possessive, selfish
& greedy person

Rings

Rings are chosen for their beauty, or because they fit, yet traditionally they are worn as significators or symbols. Men in political, religious or military roles wear rings on specific fingers, and women wear them as indicators of their, or their husband's economic worth. But most often rings are worn without conscious awareness of a possible significance of why we choose a particular finger. The need to call attention to, and literally add weight to a finger may reveals imbalances of it's associated qualities. Rings on all the fingers indicates negative circumstances. The person hides behind the display, and may be avoiding dealing with painful and difficult issues. Wearing no rings is positive. Once you know what each finger represents, conscious placement of a ring can enhance and strengthen the qualities associated with that finger.

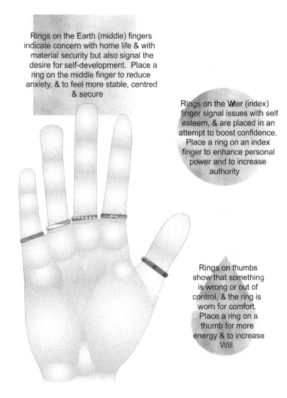

Rings on the Earth (middle) fingers indicate concern with home life & with material security but also signal the desire for self-development. Place a ring on the middle finger to reduce anxiety, & to feel more stable, centred & secure

Overly large Fire (ring) finger rings may indicate marital difficulty or economic powerlessness in relationship, but generally, rings on a Fire finger indicate the seeking for creative fulfilment. A ring here also shows friendliness & an appreciation of art and beauty. Place a beautiful ring on this finger to stimulate creativity

Rings on the Water (index) finger signal issues with self esteem, & are placed in an attempt to boost confidence. Place a ring on an index finger to enhance personal power and to increase authority

Rings on Air (baby) fingers indicate business or sexual issues. Place a ring on an Air finger to improve ability to communicate & to increase personal magnetism

Rings on thumbs show that something is wrong or out of control, & the ring is worn for comfort. Place a ring on a thumb for more energy & to increase Will

Lines

In our palms, just like in all of nature, cosmic energy reflects in the forms of our lines. Our lines express, and reflect, aspects of the eternal Ether element, as it channels through our physical self. Also, the hands hold many neural connections and nerve endings, and impulses of nervous energy register in outward form on our palmar surfaces.

Science calls the palmar lines 'flexion creases', and the dictionary defines 'flex' as 'to bend', but the presence of our lines cannot be accounted for in scientific terms. Opening and closing the palm does not produce the huge variety of lineal markings, the changes that occur in the lines, missing lines, the appearance of extra lines, or the vertical lines on the fingers.

The part or section of the line that is thickest and slowest to change, is the beginning, or Earth section, because density, consistency and slowness are Earth principles. The part of the line that exhibits the most variation is the end, or Air section, and the direction in which the energy runs. Diversity and dispersion are principles of the less tangible Air element.

The perception that palm readers are able to time events e.g. marriage, children, etc. from markings on lines is as mythical as the belief that the length of your life can be read from the length of your life line.

Life experiences that have impact, for example, a shock, will be retained as a lineal marking that shows the effect or impact of that event. The content of the event itself cannot be read directly from the hands. However, palm readers with developed psychic ability may pick up and channel an accurate description of that event!

Lines are assessed by examining their quantity, depth, width, flow, length and markings.

Many
Nervousness. The bearer feels neurotic & experiences nervous energy, anxiety & tension. Shows an overactive Air element

Few
Simplicity. The owner is disinclined to self insight. Stress is silent, deep & private, even to them. Less complex, they prefer to get on with what simply is. The Earth element manifest

Deep
Capacity. Aspects a sense of the melodramatic in the bearer, yet they engage with & deal with life's demands. Hurts are deep, crises may be many, yet life skills are strong Extra Fire energy adds motivation

Faint
Sensitivity. Reflecting low energy levels, vulnerability & lack of resources. Responsibilities are hard to handle, person may not be coping, & needs emotional encouragement. A Water element indicator

Lineal Width

Lines are either Earth, Water, Fire or Air width. For example, you may find an Earth line with Water width, an Air line with Water width, a Water line with Fire width and so on. The width adds the influence of the accorded element.

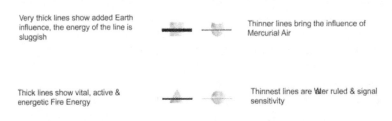

Very thick lines show added Earth influence, the energy of the line is sluggish

Thinner lines bring the influence of Mercurial Air

Thick lines show vital, active & energetic Fire Energy

Thinnest lines are Water ruled & signal sensitivity

Lineal Flow

The way the lines flow adds the influence of the accorded element, for example, an Air line with a Fire flow shows a practical thinker, whereas an Air line with a Water flow shows a more dreamy, imaginative person.

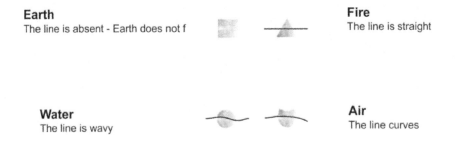

Earth
The line is absent - Earth does not f

Fire
The line is straight

Water
The line is wavy

Air
The line curves

Lineal Markings

These are the types of markings found on our lines. Markings each have different meanings depending on which line they are found. These are presented on the individual pages that give meanings for the Earth, Water and Air line markings. Fire line markings are mentioned on the page 'Types of Fire Line'.

Island
Line divides into two
& meets again

Chain
A series of islands

Bar/Cross
Small line crossing a main
line or, two small lines cross
each other on a main line

Star
Appears as a 'burst' or an
empty gap on the line on the
palm print

Dot
A dot the size of a pencil
point on the line

Overlap
The line separates. A section
ends & another begins, running
Concurrently for a while

Furriness
A fuzzy, cotton wool
appearance

Duplication
The line is duplicated

Rising line
Line(s) rise from main line

Falling line
Line(s) fall downwards from
main line

Striation
Line is dispersed & made
up of many bits

Spikiness
Mostly found at the
beginning of a line

Fork
The line splits into two
or three prongs

Tassel
The line splits into fine frayed

Protective square
Minor & subsidiary lines form
a square around a section of
The line

Triplication
The line has three parallel

43

Main Lines

Each line is ascribed an element rulership, and each represents specific life functions. Our palms have main, minor and subsidiary lines. Our main lines are the Earth ('life') line, the Water ('heart') line, the Fire ('Mars') line and the Air ('head') line.

The Water ('heart') line aspects how we relate, & how we give & receive emotionally & sexually Variations in the line show how we connect with others & may suggest something of our devotional orientations. The Water line may also give clues as to the health of the Physical heart & chest areas

A Simian line occurs when the Water & Air lines have joined to form one transverse line across the palm. Functions of feeling and thinking intertwine and conflict, creating intensity for the bearer

The Air ('head') line represents the intellect, the quality of our mental life & how information is received, thought about & communicated. The many variations of form & flow of the Air line aspect communication, intellectual range, & style of objective & subjective thinking

The Fire ('Mars') line suggests support, assistance & extra available energy. The source of this energetic support may be physical. Added amounts of stamina, physical energy, strength & vitality are present, or, support may come from the spiritual realm, in the form of an unseen friend, a spiritual guide or master. Another interpretation suggests that someone physically close is supportive

The Earth ('life') line represents physical vigour & the amount of regenerative energy within the body. The form of the Earth line aspects the material realms of health, in particular the digestive system, vitality, attitudes to money, & matters to do with our Home & family

Types of Earth Line

Short (faint)
Delicacy. Reduced resistance to illness reduces, low levels of resourcefulness & recuperative energy. May indicate mineral deficiency. The person is sensitive & needs peace & quiet. Poor endurance - they tend to give up easily or to function in fits & starts

Short (deep)
Enthusiasm, stamina & love of activity. The person races against time, & tries to fit everything into today as if there is no tomorrow, then experiences sudden fatigue & exhaustion. Recovery from illness is more rapid

Flows away from the Venus Mount
The person desires change & travel & movement away from country of origin is likely They seek freedom from restrictions of their family & culture

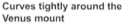

Curves tightly around the Venus mount
Fond attachment to family country of origin & to cultural Identity. Emigration is unlike

Curves wide to the centre of the hand
Sensual & responsive, this person has a generous nature

Lack of curve
The bearer does not easily accept their own physical responsiveness, & gravitate away from the physical. Personal ethics are strained, cool & reserved

Long
Vitality & good energy reserves (providing the line is not of Wer width i.e. very faint & narrow). The person is active & living creatively should be a passion

Earth Line Markings

Island
A time of low energy & tiredness, being run down, with weakened constitution & digestive disorders. An island at the start may reflect a childhood disease, & at the lower end is back trouble, especially if the start of the minor Earth line also has an island, or if this area is generally messy with markings. Also shows being uprooted, & perhaps some duality about where to live

Chain
Health issues are ongoing, & nutritional supplements are indicated. Chained at start may be childhood respiratory disease

Duplication
Adds support & extra energy person engages with life, & life is satisfying

Bar/Cross
Indicate crisis, obstacles, restrictions, setback, & blockages due to external events

Rising line
Shows effort & energies being utilised for new & positive endeavours

Star
Shows an experience of great intensity for example an operative procedure or a difficult move

Falling line
Energy is leaking. Person is drained & tired, perhaps becoming more spiritual & less connected to materiality. Can also show moving house

Dots
The digestion is affected by tension & stress

Striation
Shows that the bearer tires easily & functions spasmodically, their lifestyle is disruptive, unsettled, health may be poor energy is dispersed

Overlap
A positive indication, showing a complete change of circumstances & direction towards a more fulfilling life

Spikiness
At the beginning refers to a childhood fraught with difficulties, intense Confusions, struggles & conflicts

Wide
A wide Earth line suggests sluggish digestion

Fork
Shows the desire to travel & the likelihood of a move away from country of origin

Break
True breaks are very rare, & show a complete break with the past or a 'giving up' due to a major health crisis

Tassel
Shows that vitality is low, the person is exhausted & run down, & that resources have run dry

Types of Water Line

Starts high
The space between the base of the Air finger & the start of the line is narrow:
Shows selectivity & discernment. The person is more distant, emotions are cooler, commitment is slower

Starts low
The space between the base of the Air finger & the start of the line is large:
Shows kindness & a warm heart. The bearer is emotional & sentimental. Childhood emotional deprivation may be indicated

Straight Water lines

Curved Water lines

Ends under Earth finger
The line is short, inhibiting their range of emotional expression. The person is more introvert & harder to reach, other than by their immediate family. If hurt, they may even have 'bad faith', & be cynical & untrusting about love & relationships

Curves into base of Earth Finger
Traditionally associated with a contractual response to relationship. Marriage is for practical, material & economic reasons, yet the bearer is very protective of family

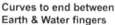

Ends between the Earth & Water fingers
Shows an idealist who wants to love all equally, but still expects a lot from others. Associated with those who express love with a fiery sexuality yet fear intimacy

Curves to end between Earth & Water fingers
A balanced ending, between the influence of realistic Earth & idealistic Water. Shows warmth, extroversion, the interest in & capacity for relationship, & the acceptance of life's truer values

Runs over the Jupiter mount to end on the radial side
Emotional range extends, showing loving compassion for friends, & for humanity. Socially active or social activists, they are kind, caring & Devoted to just causes

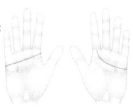

Curves into base of Water finger
The bearer is extroverted, warm, friendly, romantic & devoted in their relationship. However, they have high expectations, & are emotionally sensitive

Water Line Markings

Island
Aspects being swamped with unclear feelings, relationship conflicts, emotional difficulties or instability, depressed periods, & alienation. Person is emotionally exhausting to self & others

Chain
Suggests many conflicts, problems & uncertainties anxiety, tension or instability, changes of heart & fear of commitment. Possible bio-chemical imbalance & need for nutritional supplementation

Triplication
Suggests that emotional allegiance is divided in three, e.g. between partner Lover, & spiritual master, or partner work & children etc.

Bar/Cross
Can aspect a divorce or a break-up of relationship & much emotional stress. Many bars aspect vulnerability of the Physical heart

Rising lines
Show a person who gives of self to the world & who is torn between independence & forming deep Commitments

Star
Shows extreme emotional shock, dismay, grief & broken heartedness

Falling lines
Show hurts, disappointments, upsets, break-ups, uncontained & leaking energy susceptibility to abuse in relationships, scorn & contemptuousness toward & squandered affections

Dots
Indicate bottled up emotions, stress & a possible depressive nature, with acute & persistent emotional pain

Striation
Emotions fluctuate & person is unable to trust. Periods of overwhelming instability anxiety, fear, conflict, confusion & insecurity

Protective Square
Person is vulnerable, yet there pervades a sense of safety through their life's process. Energy is enclosed, indicating help & protection during difficult times

Spikiness
At the beginning shows domestic discord, Arguments & emotional struggle & strife in childhood

Overlap
Shows a complete change of desires, Expectations & emotional climate over a period of time

Fork
A positive marking of emotional stability, adaptability & versatility, bearer relates well to all types & is tolerant of all sexual proclivities. Shows compassion, spiritual insight & creative inspiration

Duplication
Increases sensitivity, emotional range & the need for intimacy & emotional interaction. Could reveal a 'double life'

Tassel
Shows soft-heartedness, loneliness & disillusion & an untrusting emotional life. Love never lives up to expectation

Types of Fire Line

Starts on radial edge - short
(similar in appearance to the start of
the Earth line, but short & obtuse)
Strengthens life force & adds physical
Energy, resistance to illness increases

Starts on radial edge - long
(following the path of the Earth line
for a centimeter or more)
Shows stamina, enthusiasm virility
& bravery. Digestion & muscle tone
are strengthened. Anger may be
Easily aroused

Not to be confused with the Venus Mount Crease
This almost transverse line, often
found within a slight fold of skin,
is a subsidiary marking (see
Subsidiary Markings)

Absent Fire line
Many people have no distinct Fire
lines. However even a faint line on
the inside of the Earth line, can be
interpreted as a source for spiritual
support

Runs alongside the Earth line
(From various starting points)
also called the Mars line, influence
line or sister line, indicating an extra
source of support from family, friends
or from spiritual sources. Often seen
on the hands of healers (who tap into
this source of added vitality)

Fire Line Markings
Doubled, triplicated or many lines on
the inside of (running parallel to) the
Earth line provide extra spirit,
fortitude, resilience & energetic
assistance for dealing with life's
challenges

Types of Air Line

Begins joined to the Earth line

The family environment & educational system has deeply influenced mental development. The bearer lacks independence, & sometimes lacks confidence. They honour & are very loyal to their parents

Begins separate from the Earth Line

The sense of self is defined separately from the family & educational conditioning. The marking of an impulsive & outspoken person who was misunderstood as a child. They seemed very self willed & self reliant, but deep down inside felt unsupported & disconnected from family. Independence may have been sought at an early age

Begins below the Earth line

Originality & independence of thought was restricted in early life, due to an authoritarian education or to a repressive family environment

Absent at the beginning

Shows a late development of intellect, & possible learning difficulties. Memory of early Childhood is obscure

Wavy

Shows a dislike of hard cold logic, & a love of inspiration & contemplation

Straight

The marking of a logical, sensible & practical person. The mind is investigative & suited to research

Curved

Indicates an artistic, imaginative & creative mind

Curves up

A catchment for money. The bearer has acute awareness of, & feel for the management of matters financial

Drops down steeply

The person is self absorbed, & lacks a sense of proportion. Orientation is to matters mystical & spiritual. This marking has long been associated with depression & suicidal tendencies

Air Line Markings

Island
Foggy minded (Water & Air), emotional & muddle headed, quandaries, divided thoughts, inability to see beyond their deeply furrowed brow, worry, exhausting experiences, difficulty concentrating. Traditionally associated with weakening eyesight

Chain
Continuing mental conflict, insoluble dilemmas, disconnected thoughts, invasion of thought & opinion of others, mental overload

Rising line
Show new interests, & a being uplifted by others with refined minds

Bar/Cross
Intense events cause shock, mental crisis or breakdown

Falling line
Show loss of focus & concentration, scattered interests, thoughts are Undirected

Star
Tremendous intensity of mental crisis & major worry. Possible physical injury

Striation
Show lack of concentration, mental stress & progressive mental breakdown

Break
A true break, where the line stops it's flow completely & then picks up further along, is very rare! If present, it shows extreme psychological transformation, mental breakdown, & possible physical head injury

Spikiness
At the beginning shows disruptions in childhood, conflicts & shaky self-confidence

Overlap
Change to a new direction but with the past still influencing

Fork
Versatility, judicial qualities, person sees things from two perspectives & dislikes bias, may be indecisive. Called the 'Writer's Fork' this marking also shows flair with expression through the written word

Furriness
Shows fear anxiety, person is high strung nervy & easily upset, mentally overloaded & spread too thin

Three Branch Fork
Shows strong mental abilities, eloquence & versatile talent in business & in creative expression

Dots
Tension & worry, suppressed anger, inner doubts - often related to work

Tassel
Shows vagueness & loss of mental faculties

Duplication
Highly significant doubled Air line shows acute intelligence, the extra skill of the ability to think on two levels at once, mental dexterity many diverse interests, & the likelihood of their talents becoming recognised. Excess Air also suggests so much duality of experience that they cannot focus, they are torn in two directions, & have a 'crazy' or 'wild' 'double personality', with both a private vs exhibitionistic side. This could degenerate into self destructiveness or even mental illness

Quadrangle

The quadrangle is the space between the Water and Air lines.

Narrow
Shows that judgements are based on feelings not facts. There is a strong emotional & introspective bias in thought. Attitudes & feelings are intense, possibly prejudiced. Habitual patterns are followed & the bearer does not vary their own rules. This marking is associated with the tendency to be secretive

Wide
Thoughts & emotions are clearly separated & judgements are made upon facts. The person is broad minded, extrovert & generous, & often very good humoured

Simian Line

It has been said that the Simian personality is entombed within themselves, and often they do experience a great deal of inner tension. Their Water and Air lines have joined to form one transverse line across their palm, and this merging prohibits independent functions of emotion (Water) and thought (Air). All mental and emotional experiences are intertwined and intensified.

Interface with life may be emotionally detached, and tend toward clever but obscure over-analysis. Bias is emphatic, either for, or against, as if they see things in black or white, with no grey areas. With their good memory and often astute intelligence, they are adept at and successful in the material world, but their relationships tend to be managed like a business.

Another type of Simian personality is inappropriately and excessively emotional. They are very likely devoted and committed to their partner, but they give them no space, or may be jealous and possessive. Traditionally, this marking has an associated proclivity to crimes of passion. Simian types lack objectivity and their intensity predisposes them to insomnia. They also do not realise that others do not have the same internal mental and emotional climate, and they may be rather silent and withdrawn, shy or socially inept, and have difficulty in attaining self-understanding.

Owners of a Simian line have tenacity of purpose, perseverance and energy, yet lack spontaneity. When they are focussed upon a task, it is impossible to speak to them, they do not 'hear'. Their concentration is single minded, their mental energy very focussed and laser like. This can give rise to fixations and to obsessiveness that could become destructive if not channelled into creative endeavour. A positive and flip side of obsession is the ability to be focussed, dedicated and committed,

therefore, capacity for accomplishment and happiness may be greatly enhanced if they go all out, heart and soul, to carry out a chosen task. They should utilise their intensity as creatively as possible.

Minor Lines

The minor lines are found on the ulnar side of the hand, and they reflect our hidden and inner processes. These lines are not always present, and absence is not a negative indication, although a clearly formed minor Earth line, with its stabilising effect, is good to have. If the minor lines are absent, the person is less complex.

Our minor lines are the minor Earth ('fate') line, the upper minor Water ('girdle of Venus') line, the straight lower minor Water ('via lascivia') line, the curved lower minor Water ('allergy') line, the minor Fire ('Sun') line and the minor Air ('health') line.

The minor Air ('health') line, runs diagonally towards the Air finger. Aspects of our health, potential business acumen, communicative abilities & types of perceptiveness are shown

The minor Fire ('Sun') line runs towards the Fire finger over the Apollo mount, from a variety of possible starting points. Personal image, talent, resourcefulness & Prosperity are aspected

The curved lower minor Water ('allergy')line flows over the Moon mount & aspects acute physical responsiveness & metabolic sensitivity

The upper minor Water ('girdle of Venus') line shows increased emotional sensitivity & very idealistic criteria. Nothing ever feels quite good enough

The straight lower minor Water ('via lascivia') line lies over the Moon mount & shows that the bearer is attracted to exhilaration & peak experience. They have the energy to become focussed, committed & dedicated to their creativity, but this emotional energetic source may instead be obsessive. Addiction is aspected due to the craving for stimulation

The minor Earth ('fate') line runs upward towards the Earth finger from a variety of possible starting points, & is the most significant of the minor lines. As a secondary Earth line, it provides internal stability & balance between our subjective & objective selves, & tells of how well we are adapted to responsibility & the demands of society & vocation. If fully formed, it shows strength of character

Types of Minor Earth Line

Begins tied to or inside the Earth Line
Influence of Earth qualities increase & are part of applied response to career. Family tradition is perpetuated e.g. family business, or career is conventional & approved of by family & society. Financial support from family is likely Work ethic is warm hearted & enduring

Starts in centre at the base of the palm
Suggests balance between responsibility (Earth) & imagination (Water). Shows an independent career that may have been chosen from an early age. Progress is created by personal effort

Begins from Moon Mount in Water quadrant
Water element influence increases & career involves creative use of imagination. Adaptability enables bearer to get on well with everyone. Influence & support comes more from peers & from the public, than from their family

Fully formed minor Earth line
Divides subjective & objective experience, showing internal stability, strength of character & an harmonious point of inner balance. Person is well adapted to their world. Personal needs & external obligation (responsibilities, destiny & karma) are clearly defined & accepted. Shows a work ethic, steadiness & commitment to career purpose, a developed sense of justice & acceptance of traditional values

Complete absence
There is no grounding in a traditional value system. Societal norms may be rejected, resulting in an unconventional lifestyle. Energy is diffused & personal application is not sustained. Inner needs are not separate from outer obligations, resulting in poor adaptation to societies' demands, confusion lack of direction & unsteadiness in career

Ends on Air line
A prohibitive factor prevents fulfilment of true potential. Activity may have been productive at a young age, but mental blocks to self-realisation hamper the career Aspirations & future plans are unclear but goals can still develop as the line can grow. Can aspect early retirement or retrenchment

Ends on Water line
Emotional & relationship issues, or self doubt & lack of self worth hamper the career If accompanied by a long minor Fire line, this shows the desire to retire at a young age so as to follow other interests

Runs into the base of the Earth finger
Work will continue throughout life, & responsibility is an accepted life theme & lesson. The bearer keeps active, yet at times feels overwhelmed or saddened by their restrictions

Types of Upper Minor Water Line

Curved between Air & Fire, & Earth & Water fingers

Paradoxical in it's qualities, the positive meanings associated with this line are sensitivity & aesthetic appreciation, a romantic & poetic orientation, a sensual, loving & sexual responsiveness & a love of life & of pleasure. Often found on hands of the devotee, suggesting the quest for the exalted, compassion & attunement to myth, mysticism & symbolism.

Unredeemed indications aspect the idealist who wants the perfect world, has impossibly high standards & has exacting criteria for themselves & others. Desirous of variety, they continually 'move the goal posts'. Their own worst critic, they have a sense of their ideals not manifesting, so become disillusioned, despairing, depressed & despondent with acute & persistent emotional pain & disappointment. They think about 'if only' & may even tend toward evasion & illusion, with an inherent dissatisfaction with current experience. Often accompanied by contempt of & scorn towards their partners. The 'not good enough' line.

Runs from an Affection line

Added Water influence suggests excessive emotional intensity & idealism in relationships. Devotion to a partner & potential emotional fulfilment is possible if not marred by possessiveness & jealousy.

Runs diagonally toward the Water line (angular)

The straight lines add the influence of the Fire element. Sexual response orientation is visual, with vivid fantasy & imagery. Energies may become dissipated.

Crosses the Water line

Life is spent in the quest for the perfect partner. Others are put on a pedestal & idealised.

Striated

Shows emotional hypersensitivity. Bearer is easily hurt, high strung & prone to psychosomatic ailments. Perceptions are unrealistic & restlessness & discontent are characterised.

Types of Lower Minor Water Line

Straight flow

A source of emotional energy that can be utilised positively or negatively. Aspects a love of exhilaration, physical intensity & peak experience, an erotic orientation, a highly charged libido & sensuality & is associated with physical cravings & a predisposition to addiction, restlessness, wilfulness, or even obsessive attraction to sex, drink, drugs, food & shows a general trend to excess. Bearer is passionate & has potential for focus, dedication & commitment to creative endeavour! The strong Water emphasis can suggest difficulties with the mother relationship, especially if the line crosses the Earth line. Mother may be addictive & destructive

Curved flow

Heightened metabolic sensitivity & physical responsiveness, suggesting acute physical reactions to climatic & temperature changes & allergic reactions to food, drugs & alcohol. Person responds well to natural remedies. This marking also aspects increased emotional sensitivity

56

Types of Minor Fire Line

Long & fully formed from low in the palm

Shows energy & determination, suggesting progression toward ever increasing happiness & satisfaction. Illuminating Fire influence deepens the spiritual & soulful inspiration needed to truly derive satisfaction from work. Accompanied by a strong minor Earth line, this inner spiritual point of reference strengthens a well integrated, often charismatic person. An inner private orientation in life, solitude, privacy & personal space is extremely important - even with public success, the limelight is avoided. This channel for creative & healing energy is found on the hands of artists, musicians & healers. Palmistry says that success generated in the chosen career will be recognised by the public (fame) & bring financial reward (fortune)

Present above the WAter line only

The bearer is resourceful & will attract enough money. Retirement will be enjoyed, & finances will be secure. Traditional Palmistry says that the late rise shows happiness will come later in life. Success is achieved by own endeavors, as there is the desire to retire young so as to further interests & hobbies. Also shows the need To be seen to shine & excel

Weak, bitty or absent

Success is intermittent due to lack of commitment, staying power & energy, & happiness feels out of reach. Effort & merit go unrewarded. Self image vacillates & is influenced by others' opinions. It is also possible that money may not be 'an issue'

Three lines or more

Shows the multi-talented person who is so versatile & has so many interests that their energy & application become dispersed, dissipated & scattered

Enters from ulnar side

Suggest a spiritual calling & active interest in metaphysics & the esoteric. Imagination is excellent. Person can work selflessly without thought of reward

Types of Minor Air Line

Does not approach the Earth Line
The physical constitution is stronger (than if it crossed the Earth line). The person has awareness of the rise & fall of their thoughts & ideas, are good lateral thinkers, problem solvers, hard workers for their money, with business acumen. Shows spatial awareness needed by photographers, architects, designers. Inner voice, intuition, insight inspiration are also highlighted. May aspect unconventional attitudes & beliefs. Improves the ability to communicate eloquently

Crosses the Earth Line
Associated with the autonomic nervous system e.g. respiration & digestion. Unconscious physiological processes have risen to consciousness, bringing awareness the slightest physical symptom, discomfort malaise. Owner has an interest in health, fitness, nutrition. Possible inherited respiratory hypersensitivity

Striated
Neural hyperactivity affecting the autonomic nervous system, linked with deficient respiratory action & with stress related digestive disorders

WaVy
Associated with a predisposition towards theumatic & arthritic conditions, gastro-intestinal disorders, biliousness, irritability & nervous tension

Absent
Stronger constitution with no niggling health symptoms. Probable sound health & a less nervous disposition

Very red
Possible inflammatory condition of the digestive tract. May show a mind preoccupied with business matters

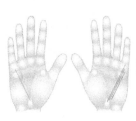

Several parallel lines
Aspect psychic & mediumistic abilities

Subsidiary Lines

Subsidiary lines are lines that are connected to, or flow from, other lines. The meanings and indications associated with these lines are reliable and accurate.

'Affection lines'
show the types of relationships that you want, or will attract, into your life

Divide the space beneath the base of the Air finger & the Water line into four element levels

Water line

☐ Air level - intellectual, mental, communicative
△ Fire level - active, sexy, passionate, volatile
◉ Water level-friendly, romantic, idealistic
☐ Earth level- contractual, materially secure, traditional

'Joining line'
a deep line joining the Water & Air lines shows a person who thinks before they feel or feels before they think. Reasoning & feeling Are intertwined

'Writers' fork'
the Air line forks, showing the potential for creative Expression through writing

'Bow of intuition'
also called the 'true minor Aler line'. Psychic & mediumistic ability strong hunches, inspiration, understanding of mysticism. A very rare marking

'Falling lines'
from the Water line show short term disappointing emotional or sexual relationships & drained emotional energies. Also said to indicate flirtatiousness

'Earth line flows to Water quadrant'
ater line runs to, or or sends a strong branch towards the Neptune & Pluto mounts. Travel & movement away from country of origin are indicated

Ambition lines'
rise from the Earth line & run upward over the Jupiter mount, showing aspirations to betterment & elevation of circumstances & spiritual or material ambition

'Attachment line'
the 'Water line runs to, or sends a clear branch to the start of the Earth line. Water seeks Earth, showing the need for security. Insecurity, possessiveness, clinging & jealousy are characterized along with fear of intimacy, fear of being hurt, suspicion & defensiveness

'Rising lines'
from the Earth line show that energy is available & positive efforts are being made

'Influence lines'
on the inside of the Earth line show influence of a spiritual teacher or guide & potential awareness of support from Unseen realms

'Falling lines'
from the Earth line show depletion, tiredness & drained physical energy. Indicates a spiritual & subjective orientation & a less materialistic outlook. Can also aspect moving house

Subsidiary Markings

The meanings of these markings are sourced from traditional western Palmistry. They are not all accorded element rulerships, but due to their often being accurate indicators, they are embraced by our 5 Element Cheirology system

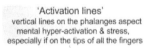

'Activation lines'
vertical lines on the phalanges aspect
mental hyper-activation & stress,
especially if on the tips of all the fingers

'Bar lines'
horizontal lines on the
phalanges show stress in
the area of life represented
by the finger upon which
they manifest

'Grille'
vertical & horizontal lines
in unison on the phalanges
or palmar surface shows
intense conflict & guilt in
the associated area of life

'Ring of Apollo'
a line in the form of a ring
on the Sun/Apollo mount
suggests that creative
expression is blocked &
spontaneity is restricted

'Ring of Saturn'
a line in the form of a ring on the
Saturn mount shows restriction,
depression, & possibly a
melancholic temperament

'Ring of Solomon'
a line or a ring on the Jupiter
mount shows a person of a
higher harmonic who has
intuitive wisdom, perception,
insight & abundant spiritual
potential

'Healing / medical stigmata'
or 'Samaritan lines'
ray over the Mercury mount
below the Air finger showing an
interest in helping & healing
others, & the ability to channel
energy

Teacher's square'
a square on the Jupiter
Mount shows the ability
to convey ideas
& information effectively
& to inspire others

'Children lines'
fine lines which cross,
ascend or descend from the
'affection lines' -
traditionally said to indicate
the presence of, or number
of children

'Family ring'
if the line appears very red
or even blue, worry about
the family is indicated

'Mystic cross'
the marking of a cross,
formed independently of
any other lines, may be
found in the 'quadrangle'
between the Water & Air
lines, indicating spiritual
wisdom

'Venus mount crease'
an almost transverse line at the
top of the Venus mount aspects
loyalty, trust & allegiance to

'Worry lines'
that ray across the palm from inside
The Earth line show stress & worry

'Cramp line'
appears as a piece of a line
below, & occasionally above
the end of the Air line.
Indicates emotional tension
linked to the mother
relationship

'Travel lines'
small lines on the ulnar side show
restlessness, dissatisfaction with
current circumstances, many
journeys or the desire for travel

'Bracelets'
traditional Palmistry links
'bracelets' on the wrist with
longevity. It is said that when
the 'rascette' breaks & lifts into
the palm, a gynaecological
Problem is indicated

Hand Charts

Creating hand charts is the quickest way to learn Cheirology. A hand chart is visual, written and illustrated reference craft, and to articulate your findings to your friend with optimal efficacy.

Begin by observing the hands of the person, who will return at a later date for their reading. Note down any actual observations or intuitive perceptions. So much about people can be 'picked up', even from across a room, before the actual palm is examined! Here are some examples of what to look for:

- How did their handshake feel?
- Are the hands moist or dry to the touch?
- Does the skin feel rough or smooth?
- Do their hands feel soft and mushy to the touch, or are they hard, firm or stiff?
- Gesture - how do they hold their hands? Are they in pockets, or hidden from view in any
- way, or do they gesticulate expressively?
- Are the hands large or small in relation to the body?
- Which fingers have rings?
- Are the fingers knotty or smooth?
- Any bent fingers?
- Any intuitive clues from the thumb, is it big, small, flexible etc.
- What do the nails show? Perhaps bitten, marked, painted etc.
- Any tremors?
- Do the palms look particularly red, yellow or pale?
- Did your friend give you their hands with palms upward or downward facing?

Now take a few prints of their one hand, vertically, onto an A4 size sheet of paper, then, repeat with their other hand, not forgetting to do a separate print of the thumb on the same sheet of paper. Note whether they are right or left handed. Select a set of prints, place the two sheets side by side, and mount them onto heavier paper of the same or larger size.

Working with your book, take each feature in turn, and write down your findings around the hand. Make the chart colourful and vivid. Use different coloured pens for each realm of life, perhaps orange for health, blue for emotions, red for career, green for matters intellectual, and purple for spirituality. Highlight features on the palm print itself. Look in old magazines, in other books, find quotes. Use scissors and glue, and add symbols for association.

When doing the reading, place the chart nearby, and share your findings. The chart makes a lovely gift at the end of the session.

Part 2

Cross Referencing

Hands

Traits A - Z

Foreword

Over a hundred psychological qualities that reflect in the shapes and formations of our hands are presented in this A to Z of character traits. I have gathered the meanings from the old lore of traditional western palmistry, and from the ancient Chinese Buddhist hand reading system of Five Element Chirology.

The study of chirology (cheirology) begins with learning to interpret one marking or characteristic of the hand at a time, but all hand readers concur that a conclusion about a person should never be based on one marking alone.

The illustrations in the second part of this book will guide you in how to cross refer the hand's features, for combinations of markings, shapes and patterns and their meanings that support, back up and verify the accuracy of your findings and interpretations.

For example, an 'ambition line' identifies an ambitious nature and the desire to elevate oneself, but it is only with the presence of a well formed water finger, a good Jupiter mount, a strong thumb and a clear air line that this aspiration will be realised.

Although certain characteristics are reflected in the palm, they don't necessarily manifest in the bearer's life personally. To give two examples; the owner of a straight lower minor water line (via lascivia) which is associated with cravings may not personally be addicted to anything, but is perhaps impacted and affected by someone who is, therefore addiction is a theme, or is aspected in their life. A second example is how an angle of timing suggests punctuality, but the bearer of this angle may be hopelessly late for every date. Punctuality is a theme that comes to light in the hand analysis. These are just two of many such variables.

The glossary at the end explains something of each of the many chirological terms mentioned in this book. Use this reference guide to learn a bit of party palmistry, to spot nuances of hand gestures amongst friends, family and work colleagues, or, if you are a practising hand reader, other reader, healer or therapist, to deepen a dimension of your work.

Traits of being

At a glance

Ambitious
Authority
Confidence
Determination
Energy
Enterprise
Enthusiasm
Initiative
Leadership
Self reliance
Will
Work Ethic
Brave
Adventurousness
Challenge
Courage
Recklessness
Risk
Sport
Creative
Art
Dance
Décor
Design
Flair
Imagination
Inspiration
Invention
Music
Poetry
Vision
Writing
Dishonest
Deception
Denial
Double life
Evasion
Intrigue
Lies
Manipulation
Persona
Unscrupulousness
Repression
Egotistic
Arrogance
Autonomy
Bossy
Command
Control
Domination
Intolerance
Fussy
Criticism
Discernment
Fastidiousness
Fixed in opinion
High standards
Idealism
Perfectionism
Rigidity
Selectivity
Greedy

Addiction
Excessiveness
Hedonism
Indulgence
Indolence
Laziness
Honest
Candidness
Commitment
Dependability
Devotion
Faithfulness
Fidelity
Loyalty
Principles
Reliability
Trustworthiness
Truthfulness
Investigative
Analysis
Deliberation
Detection
Explanation
Focus
Impartial truth
Knowledge
Logic
Meaning
Observation
Organisation
Penetrative mind
Research
Understanding
System
Jealous
Attachment
Clinginess
Dependency
Insecurity
Need
Obsession
Kind
Benevolence
Care
Compassion
Expansion
Generosity
Green Fingers
Healing ability
Humanitarian
Nurturing
Service orientation
Sympathy
Tolerance
Low in Self Esteem
Apprehension
Does not fit in
Indecision
Inferiority
Inhibition
Lack of confidence
Not good enough

Materialistic
Acquisitiveness
Egocentricity
Love of luxury
Miserliness
Selfishness
Nervous
Anxiety
Depression
Despair
Discontent
Disillusion
High strung
Hyperactivity
Neurosis
Sensitivity
Stress
Tension
Worry
Outspoken
Communication
Eloquence
Humour
Mimicry
Tact
Talkativeness
Teaching
Training
Psychic
Attunement
Dream recall
Intuition
Perception
Spiritual guides
Spiritual wisdom
Vision
Quarrelsome
Anger
Argumentativeness
Belligerence
Crankiness
Cruelty
Irritability
Temper
Violence
Responsible
Conformism
Conservatism
Dutifulness
Reliability
Respect
Seriousness
Stability
Tradition
Secretive
Alienation
Caution
Guard
Privacy
Reserve
Reticence
Scepticism

Shyness
Taciturnity
Temperamental
Emotion
Hypersensitivity
Responsiveness
Sensitivity
Sensitive to criticism
Turbulence
Volatility
Unconventional
Eccentricity
Free spiritedness
Independence
Individuality
Non conformism
Originality
Rebelliousness
Self reliance
Virile
Charm
Energy
Eroticism
Passion
Sensuality
Sexiness
Strong libido
Vitality
Wilful
Control
Fixed in opinion
Obstinacy
Perseverance
Stubbornness
Tenacity
Exhausted
Depletion
Disillusion
Inertia
Listlessness
Low energy
No resources
Tiredness
Shock
Yielding
Acceptance
Adaptability
Compliance
Co-operation
Duality
Easily influenced
Flexibility
Indecision
Malleability
Vacillation
Zestful
Energy
Enthusiasm
Impulsiveness
Liveliness
Low boredom threshold
Restlessness
Spontaneity

Ambition

Authority   Confidence   Determination
Energy   Enterprise   Enthusiasm
Initiative   Leadership   Self reliance
Will   Work ethic

Long Water fingers show a natural authority

Fire (spatulate) shaped tips suggest enterprise & initiative

Tented arches show initiative & enthusiasm. The bearer loves to work towards goals

Bearers of whorls on their Water fingers are leaders. They like to be their own boss.

Charisma loops show leadership abilities

A large Jupiter mount suggests leadership ability, personal authority & ambition

A serious intent loop indicates a strong work ethic

A line that rises from the Earth line & runs to the Jupiter mount is an 'ambition line'. Aspirations toward betterment & elevation of circumstances are aspected

An Air line that is clearly defined improves self reliance & clarity of thought

A long Fire (tip) phalange of the thumb shows a strong will

People with Fire shaped hands with dry, roughish textured skin have abundant energy

Short Fingers   Oblong Palm

A Fire line (on the inside of the Earth line) - added energy

A widely held thumb (at an angle of 45° or more) is a sign of confidence & determination, which increases if the thumb is inflexible

1

71

Brave

Adventurousness Challenge   Courage
Recklessness   Risk   Sport

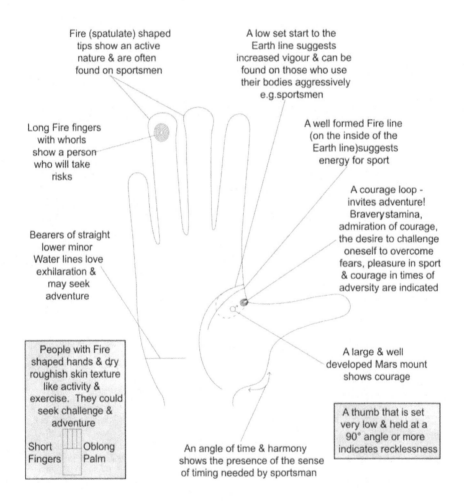

Fire (spatulate) shaped tips show an active nature & are often found on sportsmen

A low set start to the Earth line suggests increased vigour & can be found on those who use their bodies aggressively e.g.sportsmen

Long Fire fingers with whorls show a person who will take risks

A well formed Fire line (on the inside of the Earth line)suggests energy for sport

A courage loop - invites adventure! Bravery stamina, admiration of courage, the desire to challenge oneself to overcome fears, pleasure in sport & courage in times of adversity are indicated

Bearers of straight lower minor Water lines love exhilaration & may seek adventure

People with Fire shaped hands & dry roughish skin texture like activity & exercise. They could seek challenge & adventure

Short Fingers   Oblong Palm

A large & well developed Mars mount shows courage

A thumb that is set very low & held at a 90° angle or more indicates recklessness

An angle of time & harmony shows the presence of the sense of timing needed by sportsman

72

Creative

Art   Dance   Décor
Design   Flair   Imagination
Inspiration   Invention   Music
Poetry   Vision   Writing

When the Fire fingers on both hands are long & have whorls, the bearer is an artistic soul with good colour sense

Fire (spatulate) shaped tips suggest an inventive mind

Peacock's eyes show artistic flair & design sense

Minor Fire lines are seen in hands of artists & musicians

Water (pointed) shaped tips highlight inspiration & vision

A style loop - flair with colour, decor & design

Tented arches highlight musicality & creativity

Minor Air lines suggest spacial awareness & are helpful to architects, designers & photographers

Bearers of upper minor Water lines are inspired by beauty & poetry

Air lines that flow to the Moon mount show artistic & creative perceptiveness

People with wavy Air lines are imaginative thinkers

The music loop shows rhythm & the love & appreciation of music

A 'writer's fork' at the end of the Air line shows potential for creative expression through writing

An angle of time & harmony shows a good sense of rhythm & timing

A full Moon mount & a creative curve show imagination & creative potential

A Pluto mount which 'dips' into the wrist is often seen on those who love to dance

Any significant dermatoglyphic pattern on the Moon mount, e.g. a whorl, double loop, nature loop, empathy loop or a memory loop will activate the imagination

73

Dishonest

Deception   Denial   Double life
Evasion   Intrigue   Lies
Manipulation   Persona   Repression
Unscrupulousness

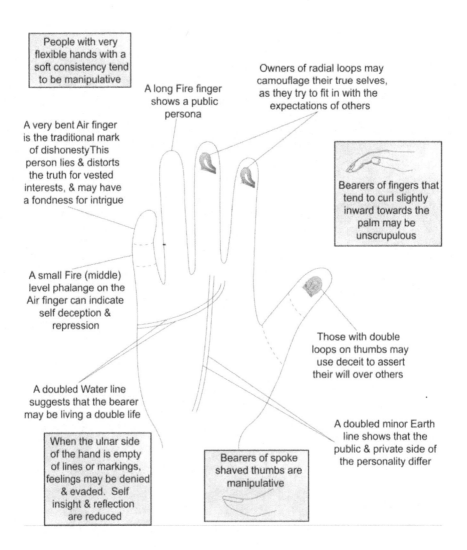

People with very flexible hands with a soft consistency tend to be manipulative

A long Fire finger shows a public persona

Owners of radial loops may camouflage their true selves, as they try to fit in with the expectations of others

A very bent Air finger is the traditional mark of dishonesty This person lies & distorts the truth for vested interests, & may have a fondness for intrigue

Bearers of fingers that tend to curl slightly inward towards the palm may be unscrupulous

A small Fire (middle) level phalange on the Air finger can indicate self deception & repression

Those with double loops on thumbs may use deceit to assert their will over others

A doubled Water line suggests that the bearer may be living a double life

A doubled minor Earth line shows that the public & private side of the personality differ

When the ulnar side of the hand is empty of lines or markings, feelings may be denied & evaded. Self insight & reflection are reduced

Bearers of spoke shaved thumbs are manipulative

Egotistic

Arrogance   Autonomy   Bossy
Command   Control   Domination
Intolerance

Whorls on all the
fingers indicate an
autonomous person
who categorises types
& who will not trust
other's judgement.
They have a strong
philosophy of their
own, & may have a
tendency to be
intolerant

A wide gap between
the Earth & Water
fingers shows a very
controlling nature

A Water finger that is
excessively long i.e.
as long as the Earth
finger signals a bossy
egotist

People with minor
Earth lines that are
deep, straight & clear
of markings, may be
domineering as they
like to keep things
'under control'

A very low set, widely
held & stiff thumb
indicates egotism,
arrogance & a
domineering nature,
especially if the
consistency of the hand
is hard

Stiff fingers & thumbs
show a more
controlled &
controlling nature

Flexible   Stiff

Whorls on the thumbs
show self discipline & the
ability to command others

75

Exhausted

Depletion   Disillusion   Inertia
Listlessness   Low energy   No resources
Tiredness   Shock

Pale, white hands show energy depletion, listlessness & lack of focus

Very faint palmar lines indicate tiredness, exhaustion & feelings of being run down & depleted

Star markings on the Water line show emotional shocks accompanied by persistent emotional pain

A faint Earth line suggests low energy levels & inertia. The person struggles just to keep body & soul together

Falling lines from the Earth line indicate tiredness, no resources, energy depletion & disillusion. Material pursuits may feel meaningless

Thin, small thumbs show that their owner is not resourceful. They may feel frustrated & lost for direction

A flat lifeless Venus mount shows depletion of energy & reduced libido. The person feels as if they live a workaday existence

People with soft, pale hands with moist skin texture tire easily

Fussy

Criticism   Discernment   Fastidiousness
Fixed in opinion   High standards   Idealism
Perfectionism   Rigidity   Selectivity

Air fingers held straight when holding a cup or when gesticulating show fastidiousness

Bearers of Water (pointed) shaped tips on long Water fingers are more prone to be hypercritical & fastidious

People with stiff fingers are fixed in opinion

Flexible   Stiff

Fingers held tightly together reflect rigidity of attitude

Knotty fingers suggest exacting criteria & a potentially critical nature

Thin fingers with 'waisted' Water (basal) level phalanges indicate a fastidious & more fussy nature

Upper minor Water lines show very high standards, idealism & perfectionism

Those with a predominance of whorls (more than six out of ten) are selective, discerning & adamant in opinion

People with Water shaped hands are often perfectionistic & idealistic

Long Fingers   Oblong Palm

Idealism increases when the Water line ends at the base of the Water finger

People with hands that are big in relation to their height tend to be fussy & exacting with details

Greedy

Addiction   Excessiveness   Hedonism
Indolence   Indulgence   Laziness
Selfishness

Pads of fat on the back of the fingers show indulgence

People with thick fingers enjoy sex & food & may be greedy

Nails that grow inwards show selfishness

Plump Water (basal) level phalanges suggest a preoccupation with pleasure, security & sensuality
Overindulgence is aspected

Full & fleshy Water (basal) level phalanges on the Water fingers are a sign of indulgence & excessiveness with food & drink

The owner of a lower minor Water line in a straight form yields to temptation, & possibly has a predisposition to addiction

Thumb tips that bend inward show selfishness & greed

Fleshy & soft hands indicate indolence & laziness, especially if they are Earth shaped

Short Fingers   Square Palm

Very full & soft Moon & Venus mounts are a sign of hedonism

7

78

Honest

Candidness   Commitment   Dependability
Devotion   Faithfulness   Fidelity
Loyalty   Principles   Reliability
Trustworthiness   Truthfulness

Earth (square) shaped tips show a reliable & dependable nature

An arch on a Water finger shows trustworthiness. 'What you see is what you get'

Straight fingers, especially straight Air fingers, show honesty & truthfulness

A wide set, straight Air finger - a candid communicator

When the Water line ends between the Earth & Water fingers, the bearer can devote themselves to a partner or to a project

A serious intent loop can show high principles

Honesty & the ability to commit are strengthened by the presence of arches on the thumbs

Those with clear unmarked & long Air lines are straightforward communicators

The 'Venus mount crease' shows innate loyalty fidelity & devotion

A long & clear minor Earth line suggests the ability to commit and to abide by a chosen course of action

Earth shaped hands show trustworthiness, reliability, fidelity & faithfulness

Short Fingers | Square Palm

A broad base of the palm suggests a reliable nature

Investigative

Analysis   Deliberation   Detection
Explanation   Focus   Impartial truth
Knowledge   Logic   Meaning
Observation   Organisation   Penetrative mind
Research   System   Understanding

People with large Air (tip) level phalanges look for meaning in life, especially if the tips also have whorls

Peacock's eyes show observant & penetrative perception

People with a of double loop on a Water finger will look at all sides of a situation in the quest for impartial truth, by 'playing the Devil's Advocate'

A whorl on the Air finger indicates a painstakingly systematic & organised person

Bearers of knotty fingers have increased deliberation, examination & analysis

Those with a Simian line (joined Water & Air lines) have intense mental focus & good research ability

More than six out of ten whorls on the fingers & thumbs suggest a very analytical mind that seeks explanations

People with Air shaped hands with smooth & dry textured skin are likely to be found absorbed in the search for understanding. They will investigate in the attempt to acquire knowledge

Long Fingers	Square Palm

A long, straight Air line shows research ability, logical thought processes & a penetratingly investigative mind

A double Air line is the marking of the sleuth. The bearer is able to detect that which is not apparent. They are able to think on two levels at once

Jealous

Attachment   Clinginess   Dependency
Insecurity   Need   Obsession

When all fingers lean to the thumb (radial) side of the hand, dependency on others is characterised

A Water finger that bends to the Earth finger indicates emotional acquisitiveness & possessiveness of friends

Rings on all fingers & thumbs signal insecurity The person is trying to strengthen areas of life associated with that finger, by literally adding weight to it. Something is wrong somewhere, & painful, difficult issues are not being dealt with

Water lines that end on the Earth line, or an 'attachment line' from the Water line ending at the beginning of the Earth line, shows dependency neediness & jealousy The person has a tendency to cling to a partner & may have desperate insecurity

A Simian line (joined Water & Air lines) shows potential for intensely passionate jealousy & obsession

Earth & Air lines that are attached at their start suggest dependency on family

Straight lower minor Water lines - obsession & jealousy may be characterised or aspected

Kind

Benevolence   Care   Compassion
Expansion   Generosity   Green fingers
Healing ability   Humanitarian   Nurturing
Service orientation   Sympathy   Tolerance

Full & fleshy mounts show innate kindness & nurturing qualities

Large Water (basal) level phalanges of the Earth fingers are associated with 'green fingers'

Arches on the fingers show a kind & compassionate nature

Plump Water (basal) level phalanges of the Water fingers are a sign of a person who cooks well & enjoys feeding others

A fork in the Water line is a sign of tolerance

Straight Water fingers with full Jupiter mounts aspect expansiveness & benevolence

'Healing/medical stigmata' (also called 'Samaritan lines') show care for others, a service orientation & healing ability

A wide set thumb indicates a generous nature

A large space between the base of the Fire finger & the Water line shows a nurturing nature & soft hearted kindness

Bearers of nature loops love to garden

A long Water line that flows to the radial edge of the Jupiter mount (known as the 'humanitarian line') extends emotional range. This is the marking of the caring social activist who has goals for the good of others

People with Earth shaped hands are kind, tolerant & love to nurture with touch

Short Fingers | Square Palm

An empathy loop suggests sympathy & compassion for others

A widely curved Earth line shows that the bearer is generous & responsive to the needs of others

Low in Self Esteem

Apprehension   'Does not fit in'   Indecision
Inferiority   Inhibition   Lack of confidence
Not good enough

The bearer of a radial loop on a Water finger may feel as if they 'don't fit in'

All fingers held closely together suggest apprehension & inhibition

Short or bent Water fingers show low self esteem & a sense of inferiority

A ring placed on a Water finger could show underlying lack of confidence & the need to literally 'add weight' to their sense of self esteem

Short & low set Air fingers show lack of confidence

Thumb tips that bend inwards show lack of confidence & reduced self determination

The upper minor Water line is the 'not good enough' line, showing exacting criteria that neither they, nor anyone else, can live up to

Double loops on the fingers & thumbs show difficulty making decisions

An Air line that begins under the Earth line shows inhibition

Bitten nails suggest poor self confidence

Thumbs held close to the hand show lack of confidence & inhibition

Materialistic

Acquisitiveness   Egocentricity   Love of luxury
Miserliness   Selfishness

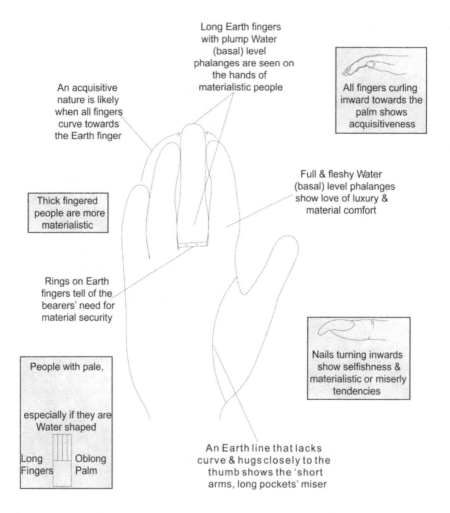

Long Earth fingers with plump Water (basal) level phalanges are seen on the hands of materialistic people

An acquisitive nature is likely when all fingers curve towards the Earth finger

All fingers curling inward towards the palm shows acquisitiveness

Thick fingered people are more materialistic

Full & fleshy Water (basal) level phalanges show love of luxury & material comfort

Rings on Earth fingers tell of the bearers' need for material security

Nails turning inwards show selfishness & materialistic or miserly tendencies

People with pale, especially if they are Water shaped

Long Fingers   Oblong Palm

An Earth line that lacks curve & hugs closely to the thumb shows the 'short arms, long pockets' miser

Nervous

Anxiety   Depression   Despair
Discontent   Disillusion   High strung
Hyperactivity   Neurosis   Stress
Sensitivity   Tension   Worry

More than five 'activation lines' on the finger phalanges show stress & mental hyperactivity especially if they are on the Air (tip) level phalanges

'Bar lines' on phalanges show stress experienced in the area of life represented by that finger

A 'grille' on the Water (basal) level phalange of the Water finger indicates stress related to food & eating

Striated upper minor Water lines show a tendency towards discontent, despair depression & disiliusionment Bearers are highly strung & emotionally hypersensitive

tension

Bearers of firm hands are more energetic

Worry lines which ray into the palm from inside the Earth line show worry & stress

A 'furry' look to the Air line signals anxiety

A steep slope to the Air line shows depression

Many fine lines all over the palm indicate neuroticism, nervousness & stress

Other signs of nervousness are bitten nails, damp hands, pale hands & tremors

Outspoken

Communication Eloquence Humour
Mimicry   Tact   Talkativeness
Teaching   Training

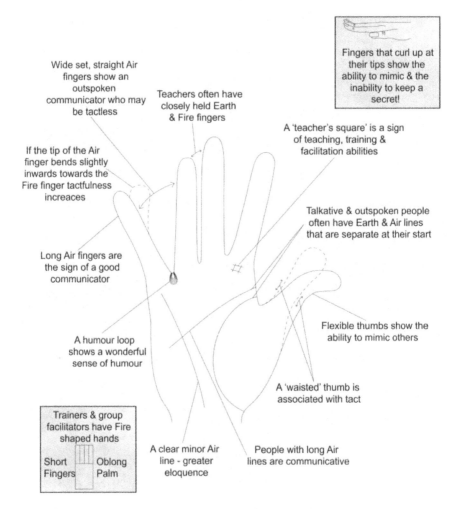

Fingers that curl up at their tips show the ability to mimic & the inability to keep a secret!

Wide set, straight Air fingers show an outspoken communicator who may be tactless

Teachers often have closely held Earth & Fire fingers

A 'teacher's square' is a sign of teaching, training & facilitation abilities

If the tip of the Air finger bends slightly inwards towards the Fire finger tactfulness increases

Talkative & outspoken people often have Earth & Air lines that are separate at their start

Long Air fingers are the sign of a good communicator

Flexible thumbs show the ability to mimic others

A humour loop shows a wonderful sense of humour

A 'waisted' thumb is associated with tact

Trainers & group facilitators have Fire shaped hands

Short Fingers   Oblong Palm

A clear minor Air line - greater eloquence

People with long Air lines are communicative

86

Psychic

Attunement   Dream recall   Intuition
Perception   Spiritual guides   Spiritual wisdom
Vision

The smoother & less knotty the fingers, the more refined & spontaneous the intuition

Water (pointed) shaped tips may be likened to antennae that 'feel' for information that is beyond the apparent. Bearers are visionary

Any significant dermatoglyphic pattern on the Moon mount, e.g. a whorl, double loop, nature loop, empathy loop or a memory loop will activate the intuition

A 'mystic cross,' found independent from other lines in the 'quadrangle' between the Water & Air lines, is said to show spiritual wisdom

A Water (pointed) shaped tip of the Water finger in particular shows perceptiveness & psychic ability

The ring of Solomon hints at the potential of developing spiritual attunement, spiritual wisdom & a higher harmonic frequency

The rarely found 'bow of intuition' - strong hunches, awareness of the deeper motives in others & psychic ability

Memory loops show intuition & good dream recall

Double loops on thumbs & fingers - increased psychic potential

A raised Moon mount activates imagination & intuition

People with Water shaped hands & moist skin texture are intuitive and receptive & will feel moods & vibrational frequencies

Long Fingers   Oblong Palm

Fire lines (inside the Earth line) have been said to represent the support of spiritual guides from unseen realms

A raised Neptune mount shows increased intuition & attunement to the unconscious

Translucent skin on the back of the hands shows spiritual attunement

Quarrelsome

Anger	Argumentativeness	Belligerence
Crankiness	Cruelty	Irritability
Temper	Violence	

Stiff fingered people are prone to irritability

Flexible   Stiff

A person with a short, straight messy, or broken looking Water line could gain pleasure from being cruel especially if their Air finger bends towards their Fire finger

People with knotty fingers may be argumentative, more so if the finger has a double loop dermatoglyphic

The Simian line is associated with a proclivity to crimes of passion. The bearer may lose their temper

Clubbed thumbs show pent-up energy & are traditionally associated with violence (called the 'murderers thumb')

Very hard Fire shaped hands, with excessively fleshy & full Venus Mounts indicate a cruel streak, especially if fingertips are Fire (spatulate) shaped

Short Fingers   Oblong Palm

Red hands & knuckles indicate anger & belligerence

Yellow hands show a cranky temperament

Responsible

Conformism   Conservatism   Dutifulness
Reliability   Respect   Seriousness
Stability   Tradition

People with large hands in relation to their size generally have a reliable nature

The bearers of Earth (square) shaped tips are conventional

Long Earth fingers show seriousness

Short straight fingers held closely together indicate conservatism

People with loops on all their fingers & thumbs are more likely to conform

Joined Air & Earth lines show that the family is very important, & that respect for & allegiance to parents is strong

A serious intent loop aspects a sense of purpose

Bearers of two or more arches on their fingers & thumbs are dutiful & will adhere to their tasks

Well formed minor Earth lines show the ability to handle responsibility especially if the line continues over the Saturn mount into the base of the Earth finger

The 'Venus mount Crease' shows traditional values

Very few lines on the palms can show more practical coping abilities

People with Earth shaped hands are stable

Short Fingers   Square Palm

An angle of time & harmony shows punctuality & reliability

89

Secretive

Alienation   Caution   Guard
Privacy   Reserve   Reticence
Scepticism   Shyness   Taciturnity

The owners of arches are reserved, cautious & sceptical

Fingers held closely together show reticence, privacy & a shy guarded reserve. The person does not like to expose themselves

Whorls can show a secretive nature. The bearer may have felt alienated from a young age

A short Water line shows reserve. The person is hard to reach

A narrow space between the Water & Air lines indicates secretiveness. (This area is traditionally called the quadrangle)

Long minor Fire lines show the need for privacy. The bearer may become well known yet will be inherently shy & need to retreat from the limelight

Fingers that curl in towards the palm show a more closed & sceptical person

People with Earth shaped hands tend to be taciturn & keep their thoughts & emotions to themselves

Short Fingers   Square Palm

A doubled minor Earth line shows that there is a private side that is difficult to get to know

90

Temperamental

Emotion   Hypersensitivity   Responsiveness
Perception   Sensitivity   Turbulence
Volatility

People with ulnar
loops are emotionally
responsive & sensitive

Radial loops on Water
fingers show sensitivity
to criticism

Faint palmar lines
show sensitivity
& a preference
for peace & quiet

A straight Water line
with a chain and falling
lines shows hurts &
emotional upsets

A striated upper
minor Water line
shows emotional
hypersensitivity
The bearer is easily
hurt

An Air line ending at
a double loop on the
Moon mount shows
a tendency towards

Double loops can
aspect many upheavals
in the person's life

Overly large Moon
mounts show a moody
& emotional nature

Water shaped hands
with moist & soft skin
texture show
sensitivity

Long   Oblong
Fingers   Palm

A very large Venus
mount shows a
temperamental &
volatile nature. The
person may rant &
rave hysterically

Unconventional

Eccentricity   Free spiritedness   Independence
Individuality   Non conformism   Originality
Rebelliousness   Self reliance

Those with a wide space between the Fire & Earth fingers dislike restraint, & are more rebellious, independent & unconventional

People with short Earth fingers are non-conformist & have little regard for convention

All fingers held wide signal a less conventional, free spirited & independent person

Bearers of wide set Air fingers quickly feel hemmed in & trapped if restricted. This is the marking of the independent thinker

Bearers of more than six out of ten whorls on the fingers & the thumbs are original thinkers & individualists. A more solitary disposition is characterised

A person with an absent minor Earth line is almost certainly unconventional

Bearers of a Moon mount whorl have unique individuality. The need for emotional independence is aspected

Those with Air shaped hands may be eccentric

Long Fingers	Square Palm

People with Earth & Air lines that are separate at their start are likely to seek self reliance & independence from an early age

Virile

Charm   Energy   Eroticism
Passion   Sensuality   Sexiness
Strong libido Vitality

Redness of the palmar
surface indicates
energypassion & fiery
enthusiasm

Droplets on the
fingertips show tactile
sensitivity & sensuality

Long Air fingers show
charm & sexiness

Fire lines (on the inside of
the Earth line) add vitality
& energy

A short straight Water
line shows inhibited
emotional expression
with passionate
physical needs. Love is
expressed through sex

Bearers of firm hands
are more energetic

A firm feel to the plain
of Mars (the middle of
the palm) suggests
Energy & life force

Large Venus Mounts
show sensuality
strong libido & an
ardent love nature

People with Earth or
Fire shaped hands
with roughish, dry &
warm skin texture are
virile lovers

Enjoyment of physical intensity & a
strong erotic sensuality are indicated
by the presence of a lower minor
Water line in its straight form

Wilful

Control   Fixed in opinion   Obstinacy
Perseverance   Stubbornness   Tenacity

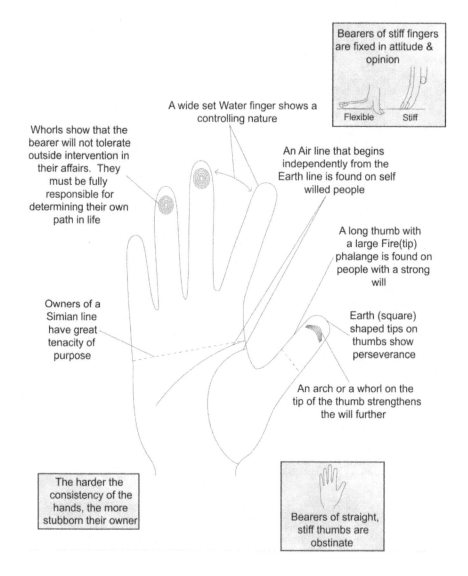

Bearers of stiff fingers are fixed in attitude & opinion

Flexible   Stiff

A wide set Water finger shows a controlling nature

Whorls show that the bearer will not tolerate outside intervention in their affairs. They must be fully responsible for determining their own path in life

An Air line that begins independently from the Earth line is found on self willed people

A long thumb with a large Fire(tip) phalange is found on people with a strong will

Owners of a Simian line have great tenacity of purpose

Earth (square) shaped tips on thumbs show perseverance

An arch or a whorl on the tip of the thumb strengthens the will further

The harder the consistency of the hands, the more stubborn their owner

Bearers of straight, stiff thumbs are obstinate

Yielding

Acceptance   Adaptability   Compliance
Co-operation   Duality   Easily influenced
Flexibility   Indecision   Malleability
Vacillation

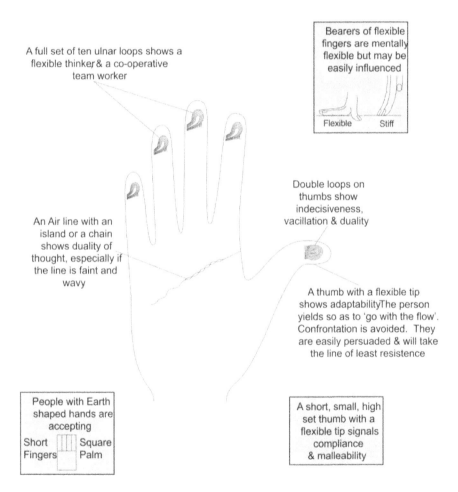

A full set of ten ulnar loops shows a flexible thinker & a co-operative team worker

Bearers of flexible fingers are mentally flexible but may be easily influenced

Flexible   Stiff

Double loops on thumbs show indecisiveness, vacillation & duality

An Air line with an island or a chain shows duality of thought, especially if the line is faint and wavy

A thumb with a flexible tip shows adaptability The person yields so as to 'go with the flow'. Confrontation is avoided. They are easily persuaded & will take the line of least resistence

People with Earth shaped hands are accepting

Short Fingers   Square Palm

A short, small, high set thumb with a flexible tip signals compliance & malleability

Zestful

Energy   Enthusiasm   Impulsiveness
Liveliness   Low boredom threshold
Restlessness   Spontaneity

Tented arches show the bearer is zestful, has abundant energy & is easily bored

Fire (spatulate)shaped tips aspect enthusiasm

Bearers of small, hard hands have the most energy

Rising lines from the Earth line show Available energy. Effort is being made for new endeavours

A well formed Air line indicates an intense & active mind

A widely held thumb with a large tip shows spontaneity & impulsiveness

A person with many interests may have lines rising from their Air line

A lower minor Water line in the straight form shows the craving for peak experiences

A Venus mount that is firmly padded shows zest & enthusiasm for living life to the fullest

Fire shaped hands with dry skin texture show zest & a low boredom threshold

Short Fingers   Oblong Palm

People with hands that are small in relation to their size are lively & restless

96

Glossary

The illustrations explain just some of the many meanings for the various markings. The glossary describes what the markings, dermatoglyphics and lines are.

Activation lines	- vertical lines on the finger or thumb phalanges which suggest hyperactivity related to the area of life represented by that digit. If there are more than six activation lines hyperactivity is aspected. See Earth, Water, Fire and Air fingers for meanings for each finger
Air finger	- the baby finger, also called the 'Mercury' finger represents 'impersonal identity', communication, sexuality and relationship to money
Air line	- a main line, the 'head line', a transverse line which runs from the radial side under the Jupiter mount toward a variety of possible endings on the ulnar side of the hand. How the person thinks, how they communicate and whether they are more practical or artistic and imaginative in orientation are represented
Air line clear	- an Air line that is well defined, without markings, e.g. chains, islands etc, which would weaken the flow of the line
Air shaped fingertips	- see fingertip shapes
Air shaped hands	- a basic hand shape type. Palms are square and fingers are long. An unconventional, analytical, communicative person is characterised, and further understood in accordance with the many principles associated with the element Air - see also Hand shape
Air skin texture	- smooth, dry and cool skin texture of the palmar surface
Air (tip) level phalanges	- the fingertips of the Earth, Water, Fire and Air fingers (excludes the thumb), represent conceptual and intellectual orientations
Ambition line	- a subsidiary line, a strong rising line from the Earth line which runs upward over the Jupiter mount towards the base of the Water (index) finger
Angle of confidence	- pertains to the angle at which the thumb departs from the hand, which gives some indication of whether the person is assertive or reticent
Angle of time and harmony	- the lower part of the Venus mount, where the hand leaves the wrist, has an angular or squared appearance

Arch	- a dermatoglyphic pattern, ruled by the Earth element, which looks like a gentle hill
Attachment line	- a subsidiary line, a branch from the Water line that runs to the beginning of the Earth line, suggesting the presence of issues related to physical and emotional security
Bar lines	- horizontal lines which appear on the finger or thumb phalanges, which indicate blockages of expression of the energy represented by that digit. See Earth, Water, Fire and Air fingers for meanings for each finger
Basal phalanges	- see Water level phalanges
Bow of intuition	- a semi-circular line encompassing the Moon mount on the ulnar side - an extremely rare marking
Chain	- markings found on lines ruled by Water, a series of small islands appear as the line repeatedly splits and re-converges, weakening the flow of the energy of the line
Charisma loop	- a palmar dermatoglyphic pattern, a loop drops downward between the Earth (middle) and Water (index) fingers. Also called the 'rajah loop'
Cheirology	- from the Greek word 'kheri' - 'hand', and 'ology' - 'knowledge', embracing all aspects of handreading. The Chinese 5 element system of interpretation, based upon the principles and characteristics associated with the elements earth, water, fire, air and etherare synthesised with the rich depth of ascribed astrological symbolisms and lore accumulated over the hundreds of years of the existence of traditional western Palmistry
Clubbed thumbs	- see Thumbs
Consistency	- can be assessed during a handshake, describes the general resilience and hardness or softness of the hand
Courage loop	- a palmar dermatoglyphic pattern, a loop lies on the Mars mount - see also Mars mount
Creative curve	- an outward bulge on the ulnar side of the palm which expands the size of the Moon mount

Dermatoglyphics	-	from 'derma' 'skin' and 'glyph' 'writing', papillary ridge patterns of the skin, which form on the fingers and on the whole of the palmar surface. Each dermatoglyphic is associated with an element, and each is interpreted in accordance with principles of the elements
Dots	-	a lineal marking, ruled by Fire, which looks like a pencil tip has been pressed into the line, leaving an indent
Doubled line	-	a replicated line
Double loop	-	a dermatoglyphic pattern, ruled by Water. Like the yin/yang two loops intertwine. A composite, that is, a pattern composed of combinations, in this case, two loops
Double loop on Moon mount	-	a palmar dermatoglyphic pattern which has the yin/yang like form of two intertwined loops, on the ulnar side on the Moon mount, ruled by Water
Droplets	-	drooping of the flesh of the fingertip as if a drop of water may fall
Earth finger	-	the middle finger also called the 'Saturn' finger, represents 'cultural identity', tradition, responsibility and stability
Earth line	-	a main line, the 'life' line, that begins on the radial side below the Jupiter mount and runs downward around the ball of the thumb encompassing the Venus mount. General physical energy and vitality digestion, generosity and likelihood of moving are represented
Earth shaped fingertips	-	see Fingertip shapes
Earth shaped hands	-	a basic hand shape type. Palms are square and fingers are shorter than the length of the palm. A loyal and responsible yet stubborn and unimaginative nature is characterised, and further understood in terms of principles associated with the element Earth - see also Hand shape
Elements	-	Earth, Water, Fire, Air and Ether, the natural elements of which we are comprised. Principles of the elements form Cheirology's system of interpretation
Empathy loop	-	a palmar dermatoglyphic pattern, a loop flows upward into the palm from the wrist, then outward over the Pluto or Moon mounts

Fingers	- each finger has an ascribed identity (area of life with which it is associated) - see Earth, Water, Fire and Air fingers.
Fingers Knotty	- enlarged knuckles of the fingers
Fingers low set	- a finger which protrudes from the palm from a point noticeably lower than the other digits, mostly occurs with the Air finger
Fingers stiff	- flexibility is determined by the degree of bend from their base
Fingers thick	- the fingers appear noticeably wide
Fingers thin	- the fingers are noticeably slim or bony
Fingertips	- see Air level phalanges
Fingertip shapes	- there are four tip shapes, each corresponds to an element.

Earth (square) - the fingertip has a squarish look to the tip

Water (pointed) - the fingertip tapers to give a pointed appearance

Fire (spatulate) - fingertips which widen at their end

Air (conic) - fingertips have a rounded shape

Fire finger	- the ring finger also called the 'Apollo' finger represents 'extra-personal identity', creative and artistic ability, self expression and the external persona
Fire level phalanges of fingers	- the middle phalange, between the Water (basal) and the Air (tip) phalanges, represent practical, administrative and executive functions
Fire level phalanges of thumbs	- the tips of the thumbs, representing will, determination and volition
Fire line	- a main line, the 'Mars' line, on the inside of the Earth line, runs either at an obtuse angle or downward parallel to the Earth line. Stamina, resistance, life force and support from unseen sources are represented
Fire shaped fingertips	- see fingertip shapes
Fire shaped hands	- a basic hand shape type. Palms are oblong and fingers are shorter than the length of the palm. An energetic, enthusiastic and creative personality is characterised, and further understood in terms of principles associated with the element Fire - see also Hand shape

Fire skin texture	- palmar skin that is dry firm and roughish. The skin ridges can be felt
Grille	- bar lines and activation lines in combination on the finger phalanges
Hand shape	- indicates which element is most available as an energy source, whether the bearer resonates with and expresses through Earth, Water, Fire or Air most predominantly describing an archetype or personality type. Shape is classified by assessing the shape of the palm and the relative length of the fingers. Palms are either *square* or *oblong*. In relation to the palm, fingers are either *short* or *long*

Earth - square palm - short fingers
Water- oblong palm - long fingers
Fire - oblong palm - short fingers
Air - square palm - long fingers

To evaluate hand shape:	1. Palm side up, decide whether the palm (excluding fingers) is square or oblong by measuring the palm from it's base where it joins the wrist, to the base of the Earth (middle) finger. Then measure from just above where the thumb protrudes from the palm, across to the widest point of the palm. If the width is almost (within a centimetre or so) as wide as the length, the palm is square. If the palm is narrower by a centimetre or more, the palm is oblong
	2.Palm side up, measure the Earth (middle) finger. If it is as long or nearly as long as the palm, i.e. within a centimetre, the fingers are long. If it is shorter (a centimetre or more) than the length of the palm, fingers are short (in relation to the palm) - see also Earth, Water, Fire and Air shaped hands
Hard hands	- have no 'give', they feel very firm. Assess this from a handshake first as well as by feeling the general consistency of the hands
Healing stigmata	- subsidiary markings also called 'medical stigmata' or 'Samaritan' lines - vertical lines which ray over the Mercury mount under the Air finger
Humanitarian line	- the Water line runs over the Jupiter mount (under the Water finger) to the radial (thumb side) edge of the hand
Humour loop	- a palmar dermatoglyphic pattern, a loop drops downwards between the Fire (ring) and Air (baby) fingers

Inflexible thumbs	-	see Thumbs
Islands	-	a lineal marking, ruled by Water. The line separates into two and re-converges, to form an island
Jupiter Mount	-	the fleshy pad under the Water (index) finger
Knotty fingers	-	see fingers
Large hands	-	the person's hands appear large in relation to their height and size
Loop	-	a dermatoglyphic pattern, ruled by Water, the skin ridges form an open ended and rounded loop
Low set Earth line	-	the Earth line begins closer to the thumb than to the Water finger
Low set finger	-	see fingers low set
Main lines	-	the Earth (life), Water (heart), Fire (Mars) and Air (head) lines. Western Palmistry excludes the Fire (Mars) and includes the minor Earth (fate) line as the fourth main line
Mars mount	-	the fleshy pad of skin above the Venus and below the Jupiter mounts, the flesh just above where the thumb protrudes
Medical stigmata	-	see Healing stigmata
Memory loop	-	a palmar dermatoglyphic pattern in the form of a loop or teardrop on the Moon mount. The open end of the loop enters from the radial (thumb) side
Mercury mount	-	the pad of flesh under the Air (baby) finger
Minor Earth line	-	a minor line, the 'Saturn/fate' line, begins from a variety of starting points and runs up the palm towards the Earth finger Balance, responsibility and career are represented
Minor Fire line	-	a minor line, the 'Apollo' line, runs from a variety of starting points, up the palm towards the Fire finger. Success, creative energyprosperity and spiritual illumination are represented
Minor Air line	-	a minor line, the 'health' line, runs from a variety of starting points diagonally over the palm towards the Air finger. Insight, business acumen and aspects of physical health are represented

Minor Water line upper	-	a minor line, the 'girdle ofeñus', found above the Water line, mostly runs under the Earth and Fire fingers, aspects idealism, perfectionism, sensitivity and illusion
Minor Water line lower (straight)-		a minor line, the 'via lascivia', lies straight over the Moon mount, aspects emotional intensity and the craving for exhilaration and stimulus
Minor Water line lower (curved)-		a minor line, the 'allergy' line, curves over the Moon mount, aspects physical sensitivity
Minor lines	-	the minor Earth, upper and lower minor Water, minor Fire and Minor Air lines, sometimes absent, found mostly on the ulnar side of the palm, each representing different aspects of deeper less conscious responses
Moon mount	-	a pad of flesh on the ulnar side of the palm
Music loop	-	a palmar dermatoglyphic pattern, a loop lies on the Venus mount. The open side of the loop is on the edge of the hand under the thumb
Mounts	-	the fleshy pads which appear to a greater or lesser degree over the palmar surface
Mystic cross	-	crossed lines which must be unrelated to any main or minor lines, found in the quadrangle (area between the Water and Air lines)
Nature loop	-	a palmar dermatoglyphic pattern, a loop opens from the ulnar side and flows over the Moon mount
Neptune mount	-	a fleshy pad of skin between the Venus and Pluto mounts at the base of the palm
Peacock's eye	-	a dermatoglyphic pattern, a composite, that is, a pattern composed of combinations of other patterns, in this case, a loop and a whorl, has combined rulership of Water and Air
Phalange	-	a section of a finger, any one of the three bones of the fingers or of the two protruding bones of the thumb
Plain of Mars	-	the centre of the palm, the hollow of the palm
Pluto mount	-	a fleshy pad of skin below the Moon mount, closest to the wrist on the ulnar side

Pointed tips	- see Water shaped tips
Quadrangle	- the space between the Water and Air lines
Radial	- the radial side of the hand is the thumb side. Represents the outer, conscious, visible and active self. The opposite side of the hand to the ulnar
Radial loop	- a digital or palmar dermatoglyphic pattern, a loop which is open ended on the radial (thumb) side
Rings	- literally add weight to the area of life represented by the digit on which they are worn. Qualities represented by that finger are highlighted
Ring of Solomon	- a subsidiary line, a straight or semicircular line on the Jupiter mount which encapsulates the Water finger
Rising lines	- ascending lines from main lines
Samaritan lines	- see 'Healing stigmata'
Saturn mount	- a fleshy pad of skin below the Earth finger
Serious intent loop	- a palmar dermatoglyphic pattern, a loop falls downward from between the Earth (middle) and Fire (ring) fingers
Simian line	- the Water (heart) and Air (head) lines join to form one transverse line only across the palm, creating great intensity
Spatulate tips	- see Fire shaped tips
Spoke shaved thumb	- see thumb
Square tips	- see Earth shaped tips
Striated lines	- main or minor lines which are dispersed and made up of many bits
Style loop	- a palmar dermatoglphic pattern, a loop lies diagonally over the Apollo mount under the Fire finger
Subsidiary lines	- lines which are connected to main or minor lines
Subsidiary markings	- markings which are unrelated to and unattached to main or minor lines

Sun mount	- also called the Apollo mount, the fleshy pad under the Fire (ring) finger
Teacher's square	- a subsidiary marking, four lines form a square on the Jupiter mount under the Water finger
Tented arch	- a dermatoglyphic pattern, ruled by Fire, like a volcano under a mountain, an arch is draped over a triradius
Thumbs clubbed	- the 'murderer's thumb', a bulbous Fire (tip) phalange, associated with pent up energy and loss of control
Thumbs large	- a large thumb is thick, low set and reaches further than half way along the Water (basal) phalange of the Water (index) finger when held along the side of the hand
Thumbs long/short	- the length of the thumb is measured by holding the thumb along the side of the hand. Thumbs should reach to half way along the Water (basal) level phalange of the Water finger. A long thumb extends beyond this point and a short thumb does not reach this point
Thumbs low set/high set	- the level from which the thumbs protrude. A low set thumb protrudes from closer to the base of the hand, a high set thumb protrudes from closer to the Water finger
Thumbs spoke shaved	- the tip of the thumb looks like a door wedge when viewed from the side
Thumbs stiff/flexible	- determined by the degree to which the Fire (tip) phalange bends outward
Thumb tip	- see Fire level phalanges
Thumbs 'waisted'	- the Water (lower) phalange narrows in the middle and the knuckle appears larger
Ulnar	- the ulnar side of the hand is the Air (baby) finger side. Represents the inner, unconscious, hidden and passive self, the opposite side to the radial
Upper minor Water line	- a minor line, the 'girdle of Venus', a semi-circular arc under the Earth and Fire fingers above the Water line, encompassing the Saturn and Sun mounts
Venus mount	- the fleshy pad at the base of the thumb

Venus mount crease	-	a subsidiary marking, an almost transverse crease in the skin with underlying lines, near the top of the Venus mount
Waisted thumb	-	see Thumb
Water finger	-	the index finger also called the Jupiter finger, represents 'personal identity', self esteem, confidence, leadership and personal authority
Water (basal) level phalanges	-	the bottom section of each finger, which emerges from the palm, representing material and sensual responses
Water level phalange of thumb	-	the part that protrudes from the Venus Mount, the lower phalange
Water line	-	a main line, the 'heart' line, runs from below the Air finger on the ulnar side across the palm toward various possible end points. Sensitivity emotional responses, sexuality and the chest and breast area are represented
Water shaped fingertips	-	see Fingertip shapes
Water shaped hands	-	a basic hand shape type. Palms are oblong and the fingers long. An intuitive, emotional, sensitive profile, further understood in accordance with principles associated with the element Water - see also Hand shape
Water shaped nails	-	elongated ovals with flesh showing alongside the edge of the nail
Water skin texture	-	palmar skin that is moist, soft and fleshy. The skin ridges cannot be felt
Whorl	-	a dermatoglyphic pattern, ruled by Air, composed of either concentric rings or a spiral
Whorl on Moon mount	-	a palmar dermatoglyphic pattern, a spiral, or concentric rings on the Moon mount
Worry lines	-	subsidiary markings, which ray from the Venus mount outward over the Earth line
Writer's fork	-	the end of the Air line forks into two

Bibliography

Ashbaugh David R.
Canada 1991
Ridgeology - Journal of Forensic Identification

Benham W.
New Castle U.S.A. 1988
The Benham book of Palmistry

Brandon- Jones David
Rider U.K. 1981
Practical Palmistry

Campbell Edward D.
Berkley U.S.A 1996
www.edcampbell.com
The Encyclopaedia of Palmistry
Fingerprints and Palmar Dermatoglyphics

Cummins and Midlo
Dover U.S.A. 1976
Fingerprints, Palms and Soles

Dukes Terence
Aquarium Press U.K. 1988
Chinese Hand Analysis

Fincham Johnny
Green Magic U.K. 2005
The Spellbinding Power of Palmistry

Fitzherbert Andrew
Avery / Angus & Roberson U.S.A. 1989
Hand Psychology

Gardner Richard
Milton Graphics U.K. 1970
The Purpose of Love

Gettings Fred
Bancroft & c U.K. 1966
Palmistry

Hirsch Jennifer
Muse Press S.A. 2009
Chirology Hand Reading – Palmistry
God Given Glyphs Fingerprints

Arnold Holtzman
www.pdc.co.il
Psychodiagnostic Chirology

Hutchinson Beryl
Sphere U.K. 1967
Your Life in Your Hands

Jaquin Noel
Rockcliff U.K. 1956
The Human Hand – The Living Symbol

Jones Christopher
Swan-Paradise U.K. 1994
The Beginners Guide to the Hand

Reid Lori
Darling Kindersley Limited U.K. 1996
The Art of Hand Reading

Ungar Richard
Crossing Press U.S.A. 2007
Lifeprints

Warren-Davis Dylan
Element U.S.A. 1993
The Hand Reveals

Wolff Charlotte
Alfred A Knopf Inc U.S.A. 1942
The Human Hand

Made in the USA
Monee, IL
13 February 2021

60454537R00066